ANCIENT PERUVIAN TEXTILE DESIGN IN MODERN STITCHERY

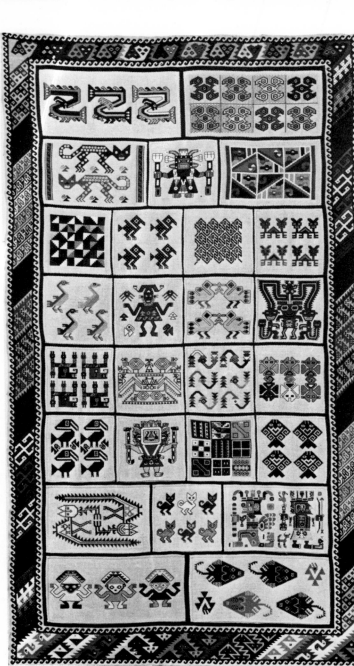

ANCIENT PERUVIAN TEXTILE DESIGN IN MODERN STITCHERY

ELLEN JESSEN

Hester M. Geegh
March 30, 1974

VAN NOSTRAND REINHOLD COMPANY
NEW YORK   CINCINNATI   TORONTO   LONDON   MELBOURNE

Frontispiece
This wall hanging was composed of small
embroidered rectangles sewn onto a larger
piece of material. The border was then
embroidered. The motifs employed all
originate from ancient Peru, and patterns
for a number of these motifs can be found
in this book.

Van Nostrand Reinhold Company Regional Offices:
New York Cincinnati Chicago Millbrae Dallas
Van Nostrand Reinhold Company International Offices:
London Toronto Melbourne
Library of Congress Catalog Card Number 70-170674
Designed by Visuality
Printed and bound by Toppan Printing Co., Ltd., Hong Kong
Published in 1972 by Van Nostrand Reinhold Company
A division of Litton Educational Publishing, Inc.
450 West 33rd Street, New York, N.Y. 10001
Published simultaneously in Canada by
Van Nostrand Reinhold Ltd.
16 15 14 13 12 11 10 9 8 7 6 5 4 3 2 1

Contents

Ancient Peruvian Textiles

The cultures of ancient Peru are famous especially for their pottery, their gold work, and their textiles. The textile art in Peru is very old and was well established long before the arts of pottery-making or goldsmithing. The oldest Peruvian textile patterns yet discovered originate from around 2000 B.C. Excavations have brought to light fragments of faded cotton material from which, by the careful tracing of individual threads, it has been possible to reconstruct patterns of birds, snakes, and other animals. These patterns have many features in common with later textile designs.

Beside cotton grown on the coast, the later textile-makers used wool from the cameloids — llama, alpaca, and vicuña — native to the highlands of Peru. Alpaca wool was the most popular, vicuña.wool the finest. An excellent quality of handspun yarn was produced with simple tools. Both the wool and the cotton were to be found in numerous natural whites, browns, and grays. With these basic shades the Peruvians were able to obtain a wide range of beautiful colors with the aid of vegetable, animal, and mineral pigments. Though the total range of colors in Peruvian textiles is considerable, the number of colors in any one piece is restricted. Flax and silk were unknown.

Three types of looms were used: the backstrap or belt loom, a staked-out horizontal loom, and a vertical frame loom. The backstrap loom was probably the most common. In this loom the warp (in one length) was stretched back and forth between two bars, one of which was fixed to a hook and the other to a belt tied around the waist of the weaver, who could adjust the tension of the warp by movement of her body. On these primitive looms the ancient Peruvians produced cloth of extraordinarily fine texture. They had great skill and imagination, and developed both simple and complex weave variants. Some weaving techniques are thought to occur only in ancient Peru.

Peruvian textiles were usually woven to the size desired, and were not cut. Most have four finished selvages. Several techniques could be combined in one finished piece. Sometimes several complete loom products were sewn together to form a large cloth or garment.

The climate of coastal Peru is so dry that rain is almost unknown in some areas. In ancient times, the dead were buried in the desert regions bordering the river valleys. The bodies were wrapped in textiles of especially fine quality, forming "mummy bundles." The preservation of buried material in the arid sands of the coast is remarkable. Fragile textiles and other perishable materials are often found in almost perfect condition, particularly at the southern part of the coast.

There have been many different cultures in ancient Peru, and the handcrafts vary from area to area through the ages. The cultures most famous for their textiles are the Paracas and Nazca cultures on the southern part of the coast, the Tiahuanaco culture that originated in the highlands but later spread through most of Peru, and the Inca culture. The Paracas culture

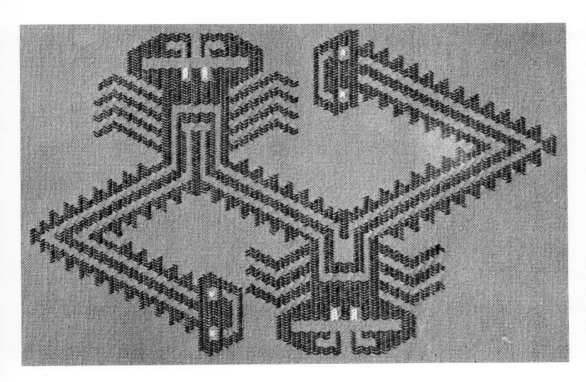

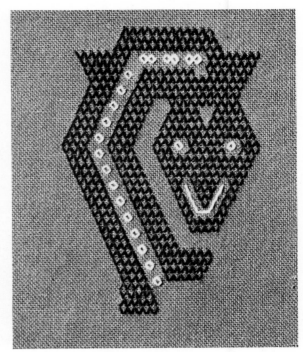

Three embroidered motifs worked in satin-stitch variants from reconstructions of 4000-year-old patterns. The patterns of birds and snakes have been reconstructed by tracing the individual threads in the original faded cotton fabrics. Similar motifs occur in later textiles from ancient Peru.

flourished in the last millennium B.C., the Tiahuanaco culture in the latter part of the first millennium A.D., and the Inca culture during the hundred years immediately preceding the Spanish conquest in 1532. Most of the textiles contained in museums are from local cultures later than the Tiahuanaco culture.

The patterns in this book are all from preconquest Peru, but from different cultures. Only the simplest have been used. Readers who wish more detailed information on the cultures and their stitchery are referred to the Bibliography.

Two types of ancient Peruvian textiles are especially famous, the big embroidered Paracas mantles and the Tiahuanaco tapestry poncho-shirts.

Paracas. In the 1920s several hundred mummy bundles were excavated from a burial site in the Paracas peninsula at the south coast of Peru. The dead were placed in squatting positions and swathed in numerous layers of material into which various burial gifts had been inserted. Among the gifts were beautiful embroideries — up to 50 in a single bundle — obviously made specifically for the burial. Many of the embroideries, for the most part consisting of mantles, ponchos, and other articles of clothing, are well preserved and have retained their beautiful colors. The mantles measure approximately 4½ x 8 feet, and most of them are made by joining three separate pieces woven in plain weave, or tabby. All three extend the full length of the mantle. Often the wide central piece is wool and the two narrow border strips are cotton. Small embroidered figures are arranged in rows or in checkerboard fashion in the central field, and similar figures are embroidered in a broad border along the sides of the mantle. This border, however, is often broken at the centers of the two short sides. The base fabric of the border is not visible because it is completely covered with embroidery, and along the outer edge of the border a fringe is whipped on with stitches that are completely covered by a very narrow border in knit-stem stitches. These stitches were much used in ancient Peru for finishing borders and for turbans. The finished product resembles knitting.

Generally, the same motif is used throughout the mantle, though the figures are frequently executed in two different sizes — one for the border and one for the middle section. The orientation of the figures may vary. The same colors are used in each figure, but the colors of the separate features are varied from figure to figure, according to a special system for each mantle. Sometimes the figures with the same color distribution are arranged in rows — horizontal, vertical, or diagonal — and the colors of the rows are alternated. At other times the arrangement is not quite as

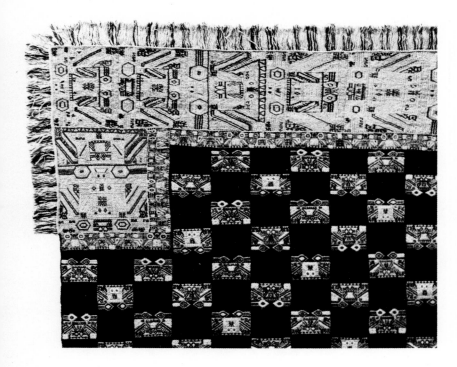

Embroidered Paracas mantle. The motif of this textile made by the early Nazca people shows a stylized and fantastic figure, with both human and animal features. Note how the orientation of the figure varies both in the center field and in the border. Museum of Art, Rhode Island School of Design, Providence, R.I.

Corner detail of an embroidered Paracas mantle in the geometrical style. The motif is a two-headed bird, repeated both in the center field and in the borders. Courtesy of the American Museum of Natural History.

is often entwined in the next, and may have two heads, one at either end. Often figures are repeated in simplified form and sometimes upside down inside larger figures of the same motif. Every blank space is filled with small embroidered figures.

The most frequent color for the background is red. Green, dark blue, and warm yellow are often used for the figures themselves, in varying sequence. What is green, blue, and yellow in one figure will be blue, yellow, and green in another, and yellow, green, and blue in a third. These three color sequences are then repeated periodically throughout the pattern.

The figures in the center field of a mantle in the geometrical style are placed in small rectangles with their own embroidered backgrounds. All stitches in the rectangles and border have the same direction, giving a woven appearance to the embroidery. A secondary border, placed between the wide outer border and the center field, is peculiar to this type of mantle. In this secondary border, the figures are not placed on an embroidered background.

The Paracas naturalistic style varies from the very simplest to the most intricate and elaborate type of design. The figures are composed of rounded outlines completely filled in with stem stitch. Animals, birds, and fish are often quite realistically depicted, but at other times a figure may combine anatomic features of two or more creatures. They may wear masks, forehead ornaments, face paint, weapons, fans, or trophy-heads, and snakelike appendages may issue from different parts of the figure.

First the figure was outlined — generally in fine wool — on the cloth, with only the crossing of the warp and weft threads as a guide. Apparently this was done from memory or by patterning after an already finished piece.

simple. The diagram shows how the figures might be arranged when there are four different color distributions (each number denotes a different distribution of the main colors).

```
1   2   3   4   1   2
  3   4   1   2   3
4   1   2   3   4   1
  2   3   4   1   2
3   4   1   2   3   4
```

In the Paracas embroideries, which can roughly be divided into geometrical and naturalistic styles, the geometrical style is built up of embroidered straight stripes on an embroidered monochrome background. The stripes are in four directions: vertical, horizontal, and two symmetrical sloping diagonals. In these rigid patterns the figures are stylized and fantastic. For example, a head usually has hexagonal eyes and a smiling mouth. One figure

Several embroidered samplers have been found, which might have been used this way. After the outlining was done, the whole figure was filled in with stem stitch of a fixed length. The stitching was done in a few different directions, often depending on the anatomy of the figure. Even though the figures in the naturalistic style are much freer than those in the geometrical style, they have a tendency to be in accordance with the structure of the base fabric in their main parts. The figures twist, but the direction of the heads is always horizontal or vertical, and therefore the head may often be fixed to the body in a strange way.

Tiahuanaco. Most of the motifs used in the Tiahuanaco culture may be found on stone monuments at the great ruined city of Tiahuanaco, now in Bolivia. There are profile views of running figures, full-face views of men holding two staffs, and depictions of condors and jaguars. Among typical

Detail of the Nazca mantle shown in full on page 8. Museum of Art, Rhode Island School of Design, Providence, R.I.

Detail of Tiahuanaco tapestry. The motif is a representation of a winged staff-bearer in profile. Characteristic features are shown: winged eye, stylized hand and teeth. Textile Museum Collection, Washington, D.C. Photograph by Allan C. Marceron.

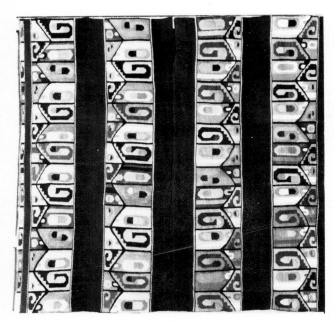

Front view of Tiahuanaco tapestry poncho-shirt. Two broad bands of geometrical motif and a very narrow edge band are on each half. The two woven pieces have been sewn together at a center seam, leaving an open slit for the head. Textile Museum Collection, Washington, D.C. Photograph by Allan C. Marceron.

Arrangement of two small motifs in a Tiahuanaco border, such as the one shown at right. *1* and *3* are the same motif but in two different color distributions, and *2* and *4* are the other motif in two different color distributions.

3	4	1	2
2	3	4	1
1	2	3	4
4	1	2	3
3	4	1	2
2	3	4	1

Detail of Tiahuanaco tapestry poncho-shirt. The motifs consist of stepped spirals paired with stylized profile heads. Collection of Art Institute of Chicago.

details are three-fingered hands, weeping or winged eyes, and N-shaped, interlocking canine teeth that are shown double the size of the other teeth. The eyes are characteristically divided by a straight line into dark and light halves.

Tiahuanaco tapestry poncho-shirts were woven in alpaca wool on a very broad loom with a cotton warp. In assembling the garment, two matching pieces were sewn together with a center seam left open in the middle for the neck slit. The two sewn pieces were then folded double in the weft direction — so that the neck slit was at the top — and sewn together at the sides, except for arm holes left open at the shoulders. The finished shirt was roughly 40 inches square, and had the weft running the length of the garment. When worn, it covered the entire torso and upper arms and hung down to below the knees.

The designs are very formal and consist normally of one, two, or three vertical bands of motifs separated by plain stripes on each half of the shirt front. Each band is divided into rectangles, and sometimes into still smaller units, by means of vertical, horizontal, and sloping zig-zag lines. Each unit contains a motif. Often there are only two different motifs in the whole shirt, but, as in the case of the Paracas embroideries, the motifs are varied in many different ways. Frequently, when only two motifs are used, one of the motifs is a stylized profile of a human or feline head and the other is a stepped spiral. The motifs are arranged systematically. Occasionally a composite figure may be repeated in four orientations around a central point.

Several distinct groups of motifs occur, and it is supposed that the poncho-shirts of the Tiahuanaco and later the Inca poncho-shirts may have served as uniforms for officials, their patterns denoting rank and functions.

Hints for Sewing

Most of the motifs of this book are very simple, and could be worked in many ways: in cross-stitch, in gobelin stitch, in weaving, or even in knitting. One of the charms of the Peruvian motifs is that they are so flexible. The craftsman has a choice of materials, techniques, colors, and arrangement of units in the pattern. Many of the motifs illustrated in the book are given as designs to work from. However, a few explanations of the embroidery techniques may be useful.

Most of the embroideries are worked on linen woven with 26 to 32 threads to the inch and some on heavy linen with 21 threads to the inch. Canvas with 16 double-mesh threads to the inch was used for embroideries made into handbags. The ancient Peruvian embroideries were often sewn on very dark fabric, but as this is hard to work on, lighter fabrics have been chosen for the embroideries in this book.

The embroideries are worked in cross-stitch, except for a few of the Paracas motifs worked in stem stitch, the original stitch for the ancient Paracas needlework. Blunt canvas-needles, threaded with six-strand DMC *mouliné spécial,* have been used. Generally, two or three strands were used, although the number of strands depended on how fine a fabric was chosen. For a few of the Paracas embroideries in stem stitch, fine wool was used. The DMC *mouliné spécial* may be used for these embroideries, too, or, if wool is preferred, Elsa Williams crewel embroidery yarn. The color numbers referred to in the captions are for these commonly available embroidery yarns. Naturally, other materials and threads can be used as well.

Before starting to embroider, it is an advantage to try out the position of the motif by counting the threads and marking the size with pins. If a great number of figures are to be distributed over a large field, the field may be divided into small rectangles by horizontal and vertical basting threads and a motif sewn in every rectangle or in alternating ones.

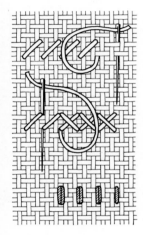

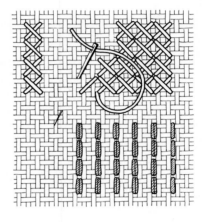

Horizontal row of cross-stitches. First, all the under stitches are sewn from left to right, and then all the over stitches from right to left. Below, a row of cross-stitches is shown from the reverse.

Horizontal row of spaced cross-stitches. The needle is passed through the cloth diagonally, and therefore the stitches on the reverse form crosses.

Vertical line and an expanse of ordinary cross-stitches. Below, ordinary cross-stitches are seen from the reverse.

Cross-stitch. Cross-stitches are worked diagonally over two threads, and back under two. When several cross-stitches or rows of cross-stitches are worked under each other, the individual stitches may lie directly under each other, as in ordinary cross-stitch, or displaced one thread to the side in relation to the stitches in the row above, as in staggered cross-stitch. In this case, the stitches in one row will lie between the stitches in the row above. In ordinary cross-stitch it is possible to create straight lines at the vertical edge of the design. In staggered cross-stitch this is possible only if a half cross-stitch is added at the end of every other row. Before starting an embroidery with staggered cross-stitch, be sure the pattern is turned so that the straight lines of the motif are horizontal.

By using staggered cross-stitch it is often possible to achieve a simpler pattern and save on the number of stitches. This is of special value in those places where it is necessary to sew narrow, sloping stripes very close to each other. The visual effect of an expanse of staggered cross-stitch is different from the effect of cross-stitches lying directly underneath each other. The

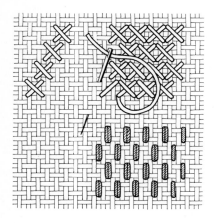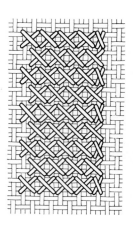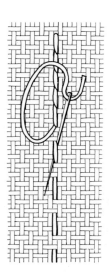

Sloping line and an expanse of staggered cross-stitches. Below, staggered cross-stitches are seen from the reverse.

Solid expanse of staggered cross-stitches. Every second row ends with a half cross-stitch to make a straight vertical line at the edge.

Double running, or Holbein, stitches. The row of stitches is sewn in two steps. The stitches made the second time surface where those made the first time went to the reverse, and vice versa.

staggered cross-stitches are well suited to many of the Peruvian designs, especially the "dotted design" found in some small weavings, mostly as borders.

Sometimes double running stitches are used for outlining a motif in cross-stitch or for separating colors inside a motif.

Stem stitch. The ordinary stem stitch is worked in a straight line upward or to the right over four threads of the ground fabric and back under two.

The stitches will overlap on the front, so that there will be a double row of thread. The thread is kept to the right of or below the needle. The needle with the embroidery thread picks up two threads of the linen in each stitch. The stem stitch is used both for outlining and for filling in. When used for filling in, the lines of stem stitch should be made parallel and quite near to each other.

As can be seen from the geometrical Paracas-style motifs, all the sewing lines here have the same direction, either as the warp or as the weft of the

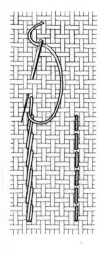

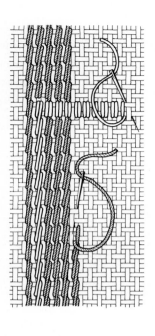

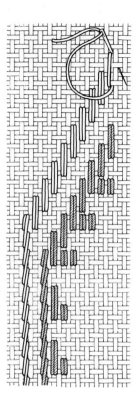

Stem stitches seen from the right side and the reverse of the fabric.

Stitching for Paracas geometrical-style motifs. Stem stitches are used for vertical stripes and for filling in. Upright or straight gobelin stitches made over two threads are used for horizontal stripes. Instead of sewing these last stitches twice, they can be sewn only once with a double thread.

Stitching for Paracas geometrical-style motifs with vertical and sloping stripes. The sloping stripes are sewn with straight vertical, or Florentine, stitches worked over four horizontal threads, each stitch starting two threads above the last. The short horizontal rows are put on later. All the straight stitches can be worked either twice or with double thread.

base fabric. Most of the lines in the designs are very short, forming either horizontal or sloping stripes, and it is possible to simplify the sewing of these short lines by replacing the stem stitch with ordinary straight stitches as shown in the diagrams.

When the motifs have long straight or sloping jagged stripes, it is often an advantage to sew the stripes first and put on the jags afterwards. When the motif itself is finished, the background should be completely filled in as far as possible, with stem stitch sewn in long straight lines. The embroidery

thread passes on the reverse of the linen when these lines of background stitches cross the stripes of the motif. To see if all the details of the background are filled in, it may be a help to push away some of the embroidery with the point of the needle in order to see the base fabric better. Or, simply turn over the embroidery and look at the reverse side.

In the naturalistic Paracas style the choice of directions for the stem stitches is much freer, and it may be necessary to turn the embroidery while sewing in order to work the stitches in the proper direction. Sloping direc-

If the lines of the motif form an angle, the sewing is continued over the angle, thus smoothing out the angular nature of the design. If at the angle the main direction of the stitches changes between the warp and the weft directions, it will sometimes be necessary to put in a stem stitch where the needle picks up either two threads up and two threads to the side, or one thread up and one thread to the side, in order to preserve the regularity of the sewing.

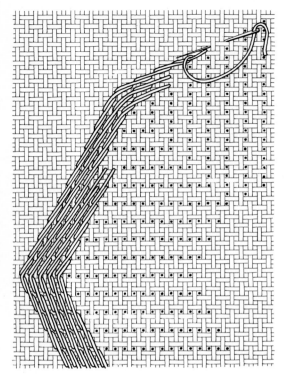

Stitching for Paracas naturalistic-style motifs. Detail from the sewing of angles in stem stitch. Both a simple angle and a more complicated angle are shown.

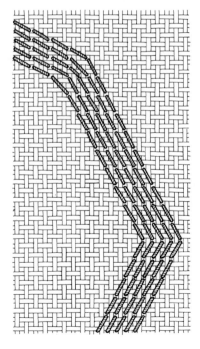

Angles sewn in stem stitch, as seen from the reverse side of the fabric.

tions, where the needle picks up two threads upward and one to the side in each stitch, are often used. The background, however, is always sewn in straight stem stitches, either in the warp or in the weft direction.

Normally, the motifs in the naturalistic Paracas-style embroideries are first outlined, then the details, such as eyes and mouth, are sewn, and finally the whole figure is filled in with stem stitch parallel to the outlining, as far as possible, or in accordance with the anatomy of the figure. Some of the motifs worked in this book are, however, so simple in their construction that it is unnecessary to outline them first.

Motifs

Diagrams for color plates 1 and 2 are on page 18

Color plate 2

1 Double-headed bird. The beaks and necks have been outlined in brown. Cross-stitch on heavy linen. DMC blue 930, browns 434, 436, 738, pale green 3052, ecru.

2 Figure with a double-headed snake collar. Outlining used in some places. Cross-stitch on gray linen. DMC blue 931, blue-green 502, browns 938, 420, 422, ecru.

Note. In the designs for color plates 1–18, one square of the graph paper represents one cross-stitch. In the designs for color plates 19–37, one square represents one mesh of the fabric.

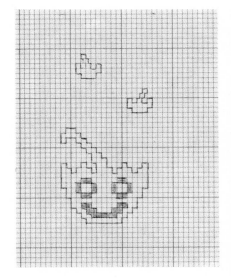

3   The two ends of a runner. Yellow linen was used to emphasize the golden colors of the embroidery. Cross-stitch on linen. DMC reds 918-922, browns 420, 422, yellow 676, black 310, white.

4   Sea creature, possibly a ray. Cross-stitch on red linen. DMC blue 930, yellow 437, green 502, red 347, brown 801, ecru.

Diagrams for color plates 3 and 4 are on page 19

Color plate 4

Color plate 3

 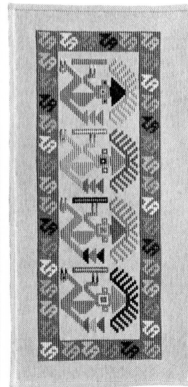

Color plate 5

Color plate 6

5   Fish. The eyes and the outlining of
the small fish in the center field are in
the same color as the background in the
borders. Cross-stitch on light yellow linen.
DMC blues 930, 932, browns 938, 435,
739, red 355.

6   Four cormorants. Cross-stitch on gray
linen. DMC yellow 437, red 356, blue 932,
brown 801.

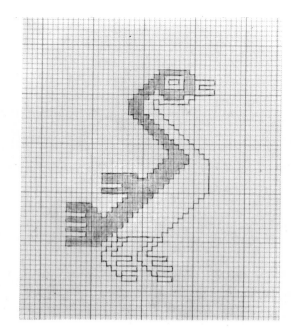

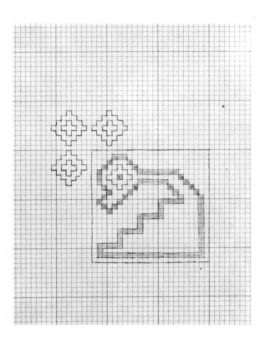

7 Figures in a geometrical design. The same four colors are used in all the figures on this napkin. Cross-stitch on light yellow linen. DMC light brown 680, red 919, light gray 822, blue 930.

8 Birds in a geometrical design. If only three different colors, instead of four, had been chosen for the birds and their backgrounds, the color distribution would have been the same in all four sides of the square. Cross-stitch on light yellow linen. DMC yellow 437, blue 931, beige 739, lilac 550, black 310, brown 433, red-yellow 922.

9 Bag sewn on double mesh canvas with 16 double-mesh threads to the inch. Cross-stitch. DMC reds 3350, 3354, blue 931, browns 938, 869, 420, 422, ecru.

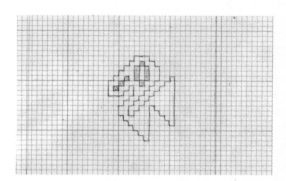

Diagrams for color plates 7, 8, and 9 are on page 23

Color plate 8

Color plate 7

Color plate 9

Diagrams for color plates 10 and 11 are on page 26

Color plate 10

Color plate 11

10   This design was taken from a
Tiahuanaco vase painting. Outlining in
black. Cross-stitch on gray linen. DMC
red 355, black 310, gray 642, yellow 437,
white.

11   Two figures from a Tiahuanaco
tapestry. One figure has a winged eye.
Double running stitch used for separating
colors. Cross-stitch on gray linen. DMC
black 310, red 347, light red 224, browns
801, 420, 422, gray 642, blue 932, white.

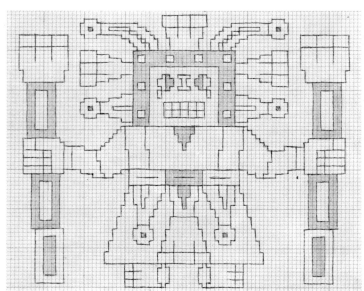

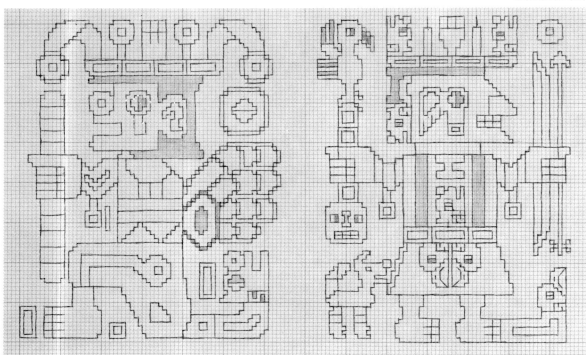

12 This figure has many features in common with the running figures on the Sun Gate in Tiahuanaco. Cross-stitch on linen. DMC blue 798, red 347, green 367, yellow 738.

13 Detail of running figure.

Diagrams for color plates 12 and 13 are on page 27

Color plate 12

Color plate 13

Color plate 14

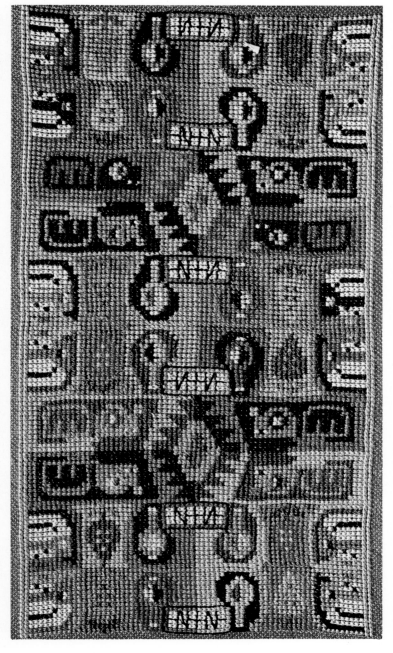

Diagrams for color plates 14 and 15 are on page 30

Color plate 15

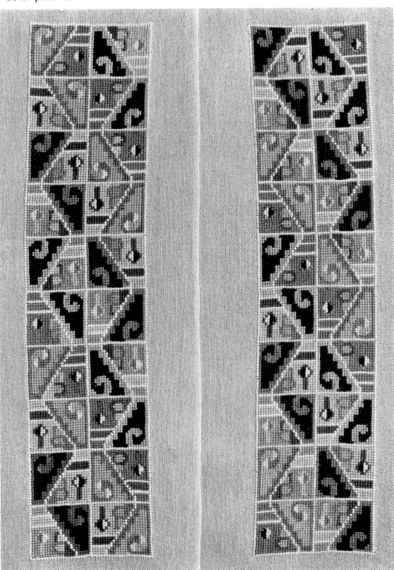

14 In this Tiahuanaco border the main colors are repeated crosswise around centers in the vertical axis. Motifs on the outer edges are birds' heads with big white beaks. Cross-stitch on linen. DMC black 310, reds 221, 347, 3328, 760, blue 798, greens 470, 732, 832, brown 433, yellows 729, 676, 437, white.

15 The easiest way to work Tiahuanaco borders like these is by beginning with the white framework. When the frame is finished, the motifs are put in. The two small motifs have three color distributions each. Cross-stitch on gray linen. DMC blue 798, gray 640, reds 355, 758, beige 738, 422, brown 300, black 310, white.

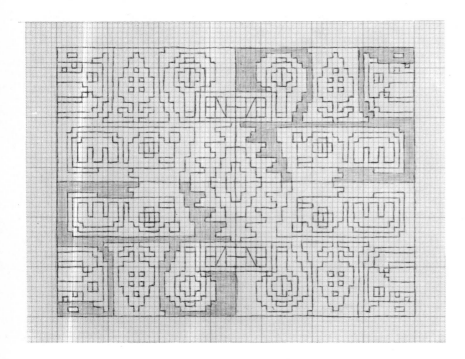

16 In these Tiahuanaco borders colors
are repeated crosswise around centers in
the vertical axis. Cross-stitch on linen.
DMC blue 322, reds 355, 356, browns 938,
436, 300, 632, 407, 950, yellow 437, lilac
224, white.

17 Each of the two small design units
in these Tiahuanaco borders has two
forms, a broad form for the units nearest
the wide center stripe, and a narrow form
for the outer units. Cross-stitch on light
yellow linen. DMC blue 930, black 310,
browns 434-437, 738, 739, ecru.

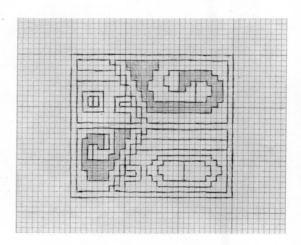

Diagrams for color plates 16 and 17 are on page 31

Color plate 16

Color plate 17

Color plate 19

18 Most of the embroidery in this Paracas design was done in ordinary cross-stitch, only the heads of the snakes and some details of the smaller animals are in staggered cross-stitch. DMC black 310, yellow 402, green 3011, blue 930, red 347, brown 632, white. Detail c of the diagram is shown double size relative to the other parts.

19 Doily with Paracas bird design. DMC yellow 833, green 320, blue 797.

Starting with the upper part of the bird's head, the head and body are worked in ordinary cross-stitch, but the beak is omitted until later. The body is worked to a total width of only seven stitches, i.e., two stitches on either side of the neck. On each shoulder there is one stitch worked at half the height of the others. When seven rows of body have been worked, the tail and the tail-feathers are then worked in staggered cross-stitch. Then the embroidery is turned sideways, and the beak and wings are sewn, also in staggered cross-stitch. The individual stitches are always worked so that the over stitch of each cross-stitch passes from the lower right-hand corner to the upper left. Since the embroidery is turned on edge before starting the wings, the over stitches on the body run in a different direction from those on the wings, thus providing a more interesting visual effect in the sewing.

The right side of the diagram shows where to put in additional colors, if more than one color is used in each bird. It also indicates how the tips of the wings meet if four birds are arranged in a circle, either with the heads or with the tails toward the center.

a

b
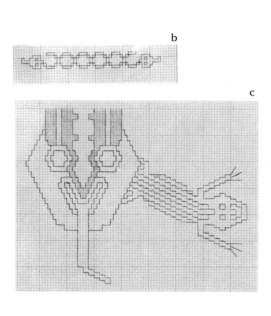

c

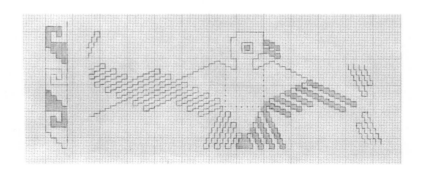

20 Doily with wild animal surrounded by birds. Staggered cross-stitch on linen. DMC red 919, blue-green 924, browns 420, 422, 738, ecru.

21 Four sitting figures. Ordinary and staggered cross-stitch on linen. DMC red 920, yellow 437, green 502, blues 930, 932, brown 433.

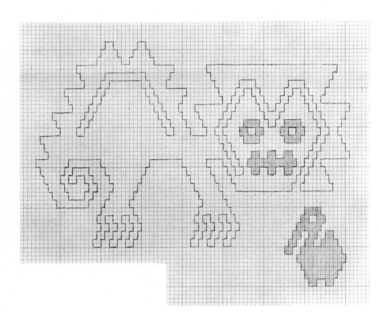

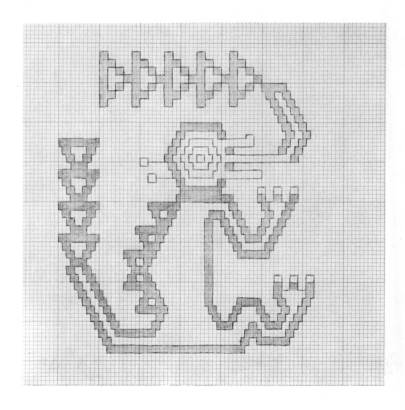

Diagrams for color plates 20 and 21 are on page 35

Color plate 20

Color plate 21

Diagrams for color plates 22 and 23 are on page 38

Color plate 22

Color plate 23

22   Detail of napkin with motifs of sea
creatures. Staggered cross-stitch on yellow
linen. DMC green 470, blue 932, browns
738, 739, 436, 437, 433, 801, ecru. See
diagram 2 on page 18 for border motif.

23   In each of these three motifs the three
colors may be placed in six different
ways. Staggered cross-stitch on heavy
gray linen. DMC dark gray 844, red 3328,
yellow 437.

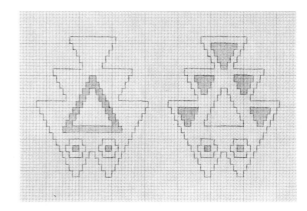

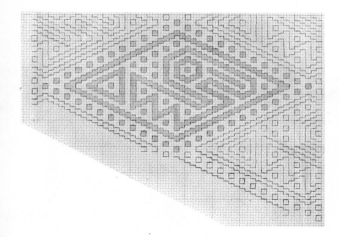

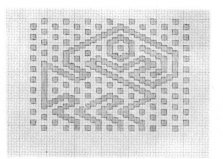

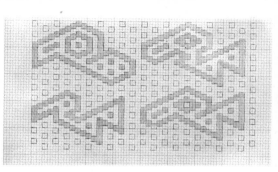

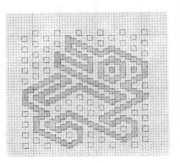

24 *Left.* Napkin holder. First the "dotted design" was worked all in dark red. DMC red 355, light red 760, yellows 437, 739, black 310, green 731.

Right. Border with four-headed birds. First the whole design is worked in dark red with staggered cross-stitch except for the long outer edges of the border, where the cross-stitches lie directly under each other. Start with a solid row of 29 cross-stitches, forming one end of the border. DMC dark red 918, light red 356, brown 435, yellow 437, green 730, ecru.

25 A small bag. Staggered cross-stitch on linen. The narrow sloping borders in the "dotted design" are often used as they are here, in different colors and sloping toward each other. DMC black 310, gray 640, green 367, red 919, yellow 437, blue 930, white.

26 Different ways of varying the filling in of a "dotted design." DMC red 347, light red 760, orange 402, yellow 437, green-brown 830, brown 434.

27 Narrow border with birds surrounding a small animal. The "dotted design" is all in dark brown. DMC dark brown 938, brown 420, beige 422, red 919, ecru.

Diagrams for color plates 24, 25, 26, and 27 are on page 39

Color plate 25

Color plate 24

Color plate 26

Color plate 27

Diagrams for color plates 28 and 29 are on page 42

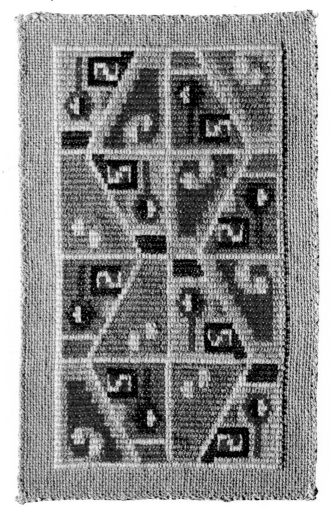

Color plate 28

Color plate 29

28 Tiahuanaco border. Straight gobelin stitches over two threads on heavy linen. All six strands of the yarn were used. DMC red 347, light red 3328, blue 518, brown 433, black 310, gray 612, dark yellow 976, yellow 437, beige 738, white.

29 Figure in geometrical Paracas style. Stem stitch on linen. Only the inside of the figure is filled in. DMC red 347, yellow 437, green 501, blue 930.

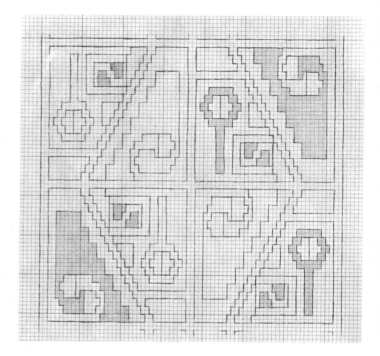

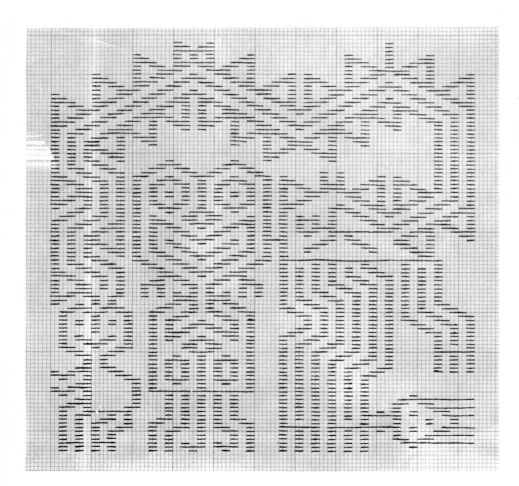

30 Detail of mask motifs and border of wall hanging.

It has been necessary to divide this pattern into two parts. The point of juncture is indicated by large arrows. The vertical axis in the small picture shows where the motif was divided, and between the two other vertical lines (on the pattern and on the small picture) lies the entire pattern, since the design for further sewing is obtained by turning the pattern around and repeating it.

31 Detail of bird motif on corner square of wall hanging.

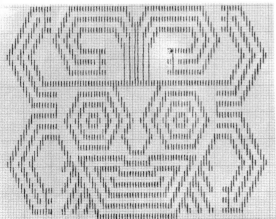

32 Wall hanging in Paracas geometrical style. Stem stitch in wool on gray linen. All four colors were used in different color distributions in each mask. EW red 2-1, yellow 3-1, green 4-1, blue 5-1.

Diagrams for color plates 30, 31, and 32 are on page 43

Color plate 31

Color plate 30

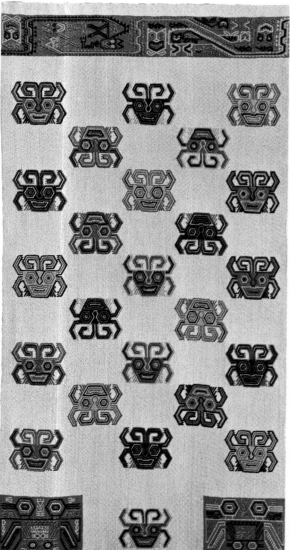

Color plate 32

Diagrams for color plates 33, 34, and 35 are on page 46

Color plate 33

Color plate 34

Color plate 35

33 Wall hanging in naturalistic Paracas
style. (The center field has been folded
under to bring the lower border into
view.) Stem stitch in wool on gray linen.
First the condors are sewn in a solid color,
except for the eyes, or with a second color
for the middle line of the wing feathers.
The red condor in the center field is
outlined in yellow stem stitch when
finished, and each condor in the border
is outlined in its own body color, if
outlining is needed.

The fish are outlined first, using the main
color to delineate body and fins. Then
the mouth, eyebrows, and outer stripe
are sewn in a second color, and the eyes
and inner stripe in a third color. Finally,
the remaining parts are filled in with the
main color, which was originally used
for outlining. Sewing the curves in these
fish motifs has a tendency to pull the
linen out of shape, and careful ironing
is needed when the hanging is finished.
EW red 2-1, yellow 3-1, green 4-1, blue 5-1.

34 Detail of fish motif in center field
of wall hanging.

35 Wall hanging with flying condors.
Stem stitch in fine wool on heavy gray
linen. Each bird may be sewn in a solid
color, except for the eye and the beak-
line. On this wall hanging, however, the
legs and the middle lines of the feathers
of the wings and tail have been sewn in a
second color. This second color has been
used for outlining the head, neck, and
eye. EW red 2-1, yellow 3-1, light yellow
11-4, light green 10-3.

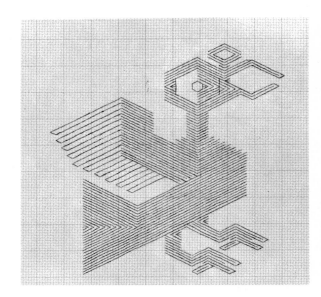

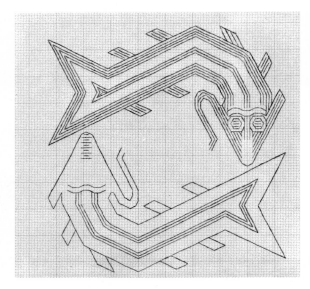

36 Two-headed bird in geometrical Paracas style. Stem stitch on linen. DMC red 347, yellow 437, green 367, blue 930, brown 839. The contour of the bird is shown on the left half of the diagram.

37 This figure may be considered either as a falling figure or as a dancing figure depending on how it is turned. Stem stitch with a single strand of thread on fine white linen. First the contour was sewn in red, then the details were worked in different colors, and finally the whole figure was filled in with green stem stitch. The lines of stem stitch follow the outer form of the figure as closely as possible. The color change seen at the knees and elbows is caused by the change in the direction of the stitches. DMC red 919, black 310, blue 931, yellow 676, green 3052.

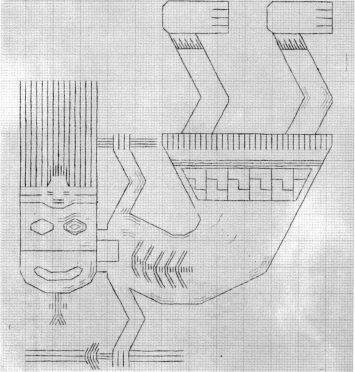

Diagrams for color plates 36 and 37 are on page 47

Color plate 36

Color plate 37

Additional Diagrams

BORDERS

1 Border in Paracas geometrical style. Mostly staggered cross-stitch on coarse red sackcloth, or burlap. DMC blue 336, yellow 437, green 3011.

2 Paracas border. Staggered cross-stitch on linen. DMC blue 930, yellow 729, red 355, green 367.

3 Double-headed snakes. Three colors are alternated: what is yellow in the first group of figures is blue in the second group and green in the third. In the same way, what is yellow in the second group will be blue in the third group and green in the first. Cross-stitch on red linen. DMC yellow 437, green 501, blue 939.

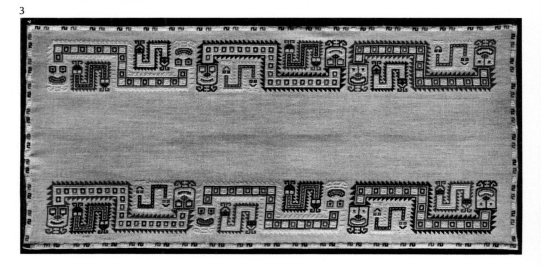

50

One square of the graph paper represents one mesh of the fabric.

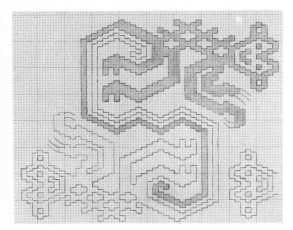

One square of the graph paper represents one mesh of the fabric.

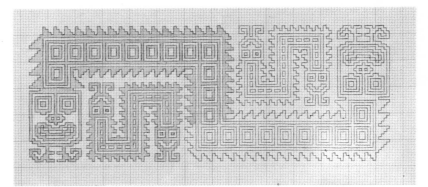

One square of the graph paper represents one cross-stitch.

ANIMALS

1   Eight small dogs. Hold the pattern sideway when sewing. Staggered cross-stitch on linen. DMC yellow 437, red 919, blue 930, green 502.

2   Eight dogs in a circle. Staggered cross-stitch on linen. DMC yellow 437, red 919, green 367, blue 312, lilac 327, brown 839.

3   Four dogs in a circle. Warm and cool colors are alternated. The red and yellow dogs have blue or green eyes and vice versa. DMC red 920, yellow 676, green 320, blue 312.

1

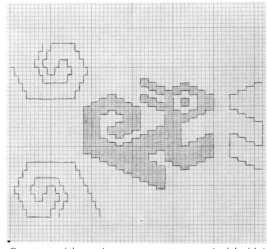

One square of the graph paper represents one mesh of the fabric.

2

3

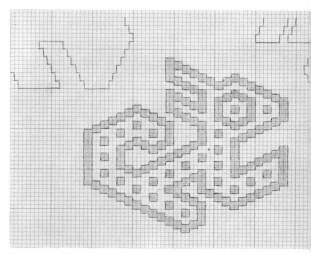

One square of the graph paper represents one mesh of the fabric.

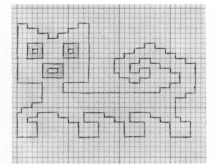

One square of the graph paper
represents one cross-stitch.

One square of the graph paper
represents one cross-stitch.

One square of the graph paper
represents one cross-stitch.

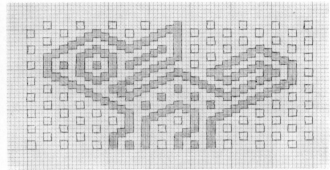

One square of the graph paper represents one mesh of the fabric.

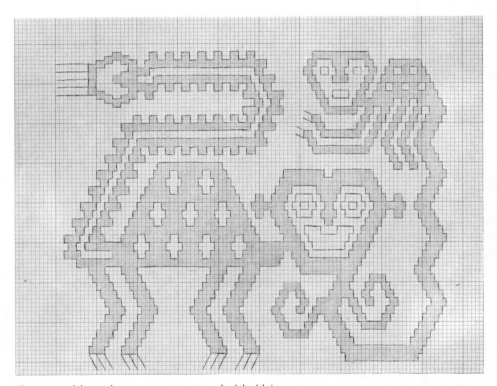

One square of the graph paper represents one mesh of the fabric.

One square of the graph paper
represents one mesh of the fabric.

BIRDS

1 Birds. Turn this pattern sideway when sewing. Staggered cross-stitch on linen. DMC green 3052, yellow 436, gray 644, red 356.

2 Bird. First sew the bird in staggered cross-stitch, holding the pattern sideway. Then outline it and separate the wing feathers in another color in double running stitches. DMC green 501, red 919, yellow 437.

One square of the graph paper represents one mesh of the fabric.

One square of the graph paper represents one mesh of the fabric.

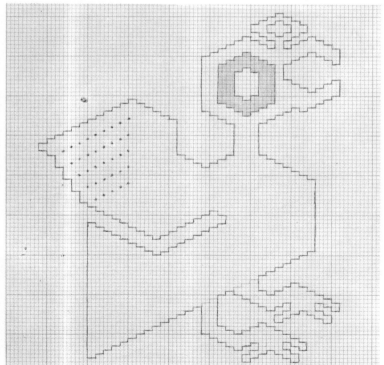

1

2

54

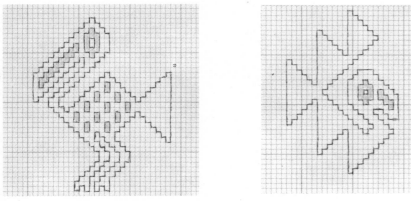

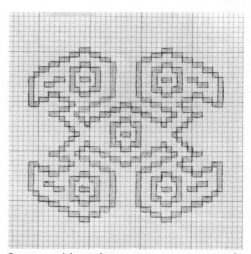

One square of the graph paper represents one cross-stitch.

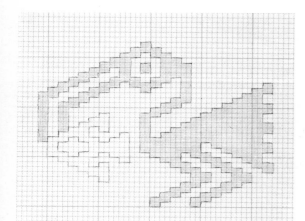

One square of the graph paper represents one mesh of the fabric.

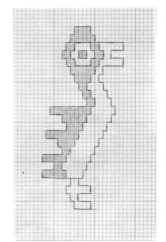

One square of the graph paper represents
one mesh of the fabric.

One square of the graph paper represents one cross-stitch.

FIGURES

1 Paracas figure. This figure holds a knife in one hand and a lance in the other. From the side of the head issues a long, broad appendage, and a bird is tied to the top of the head. Mostly staggered cross-stitch. DMC red 347, light red 761, blue 311, light blue 932, olive greens 3011, 3012, browns 420, 422.

2 Doily with three figures. Mostly staggered cross-stitch. DMC red 919, yellow 422, brown 839.

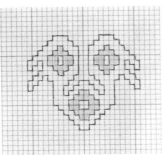

One square of the graph paper represents one cross-stitch.

1

One square of the graph paper represents one mesh of the fabric.

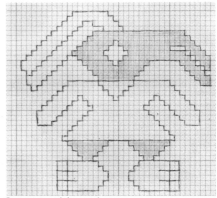

One square of the graph paper represents one cross-stitch.

2

One square of the graph paper
represents one mesh of the fabric.

3 Stylized figure. This is actually a highly stylized male condor. Cross-stitch on linen. DMC blue 930, red 347, olive-green 730, oranges 402, 301, brown 300, beige 422.

4 Doily with four figures. Staggered cross-stitch on linen. DMC red 356, blue 930, green 501, yellow 437.

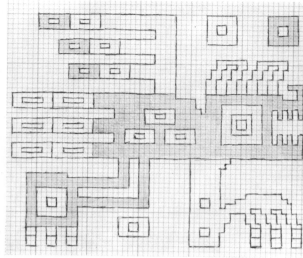

One square of the graph paper represents one cross-stitch.

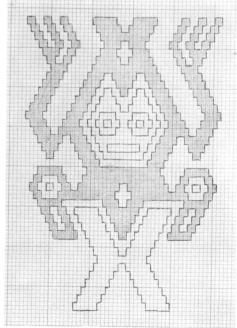

One square of the graph paper represents one mesh of the fabric.

GEOMETRICAL PATTERNS

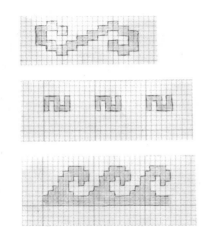

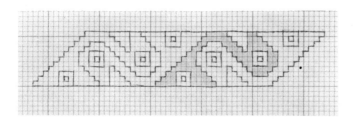

One square of the graph paper represents one cross-stitch.

1 Doily. Cross-stitch on linen. DMC red
349, brown 300, green 470, blue 931,
orange-yellow 402.

One square of the **graph paper represents** one mesh of the fabric.

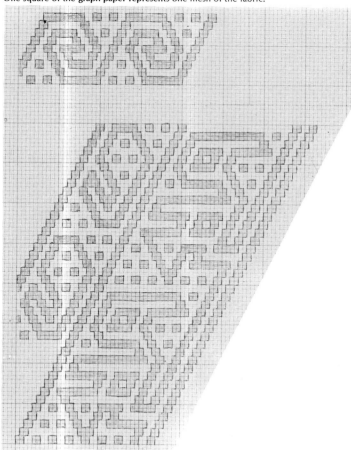

1

One square of the graph paper represents one cross-stitch.

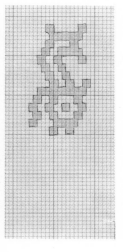

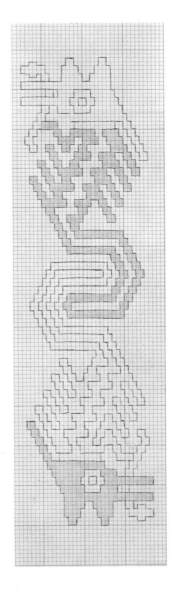

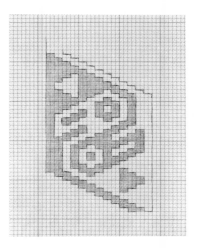

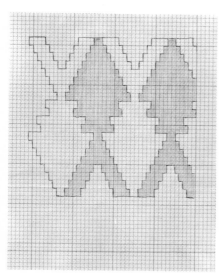

One square of the graph paper represents one mesh of the fabric.

2 Two bookmarks. These two simple designs were made in running·stitch, and can be viewed from either side.

3 Reverse sides of the bookmarks.

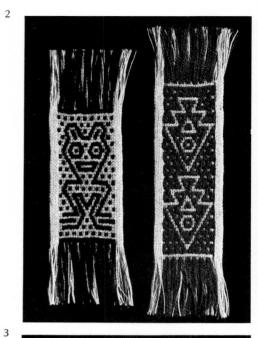

One square of the graph paper represents one mesh of the fabric.

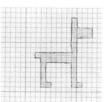

One square of the graph paper represents one cross-stitch.

Bibliography

FURTHER PATTERNS

Bibliothèque DMC. *Motifs précolumbiens*. Editions Th. de Dillmont. Mulhouse (France). This book contains Peruvian patterns in color, mostly borders.

Jessen, Ellen. *Gamle motiver til Korssting fra Peru*. Høst & Søns Forlag, Copenhagen, 1966. Text in Danish and English. Gives color numbers for the yarns.

GENERAL READING

Bennett, Wendell C. *Ancient Art of the Andes*. The Museum of Modern Art, New York, 1954. Reprint edition 1966, Arno Press. 188 pp. in 7½" x 10" format. An inspiring book. Numerous illustrations.

Bird, Junius and Bellinger, Louisa. *Paracas Fabrics and Nazca Needlework*, Textile Museum Catalogue Raisonné. National Publishing, Washington, D.C., 1954. 126 pp. and 127 plates — 16 in color — 9" x 12" format. Very informative and very well illustrated.

D'Harcourt, Raoul. *Textiles of Ancient Peru and their Techniques*. University of Washington Press, Seattle, 1962. 186 pp. and 121 plates — 4 in color — 9" x 12" format. Very thorough. Well illustrated. For specialists.

King, Mary Elizabeth. *Ancient Peruvian Textiles from the Collection of The Textile Museum Washington D.C.* The Museum of Primitive Art, New York, 1965. Distributed by New York Graphic Society. 48 pp. in 8½" x format. A clear, illustrated survey of ancient Peruvian textiles.

Mason, J. Aldon. *The Ancient Civilizations of Peru*. Pelican Books, Penguin 1957. 330 pp. and 64 plates in 4½" x 7" format. Very informative.

Sawyer, Alan R. *Tiahuanaco Tapestry Design*. Study 3. The Museum of Primitive Art, 1963. Distributed by New York Graphic Society. Simultaneously published in The Textile Museum Journal vol. 1, No. 2 (December, 196 12 pp. in 8½" x 11" format. A discussion of the development of Tiahuanaco weaving designs.

Sawyer, Alan R. *Mastercraftsmen of Ancient Peru*, Exhibition catalog. The Solomon R. Guggenheim Foundation, New York, 1968. 112 pp. in 7½" x 11" format. Numerous illustrations, many in color. Includes recent archaeological findings.

Van Stan, I. *The Fabrics of Peru*. F. Lewis Ltd., Leigh-on-Sea, England, 19 16 pp. and 48 plates in 8½" x 11" format. Treats textiles from late Peruvian cultures.

One flag, one land,
one heart, one hand,
One Nation, "Evermore!"

Independence Day

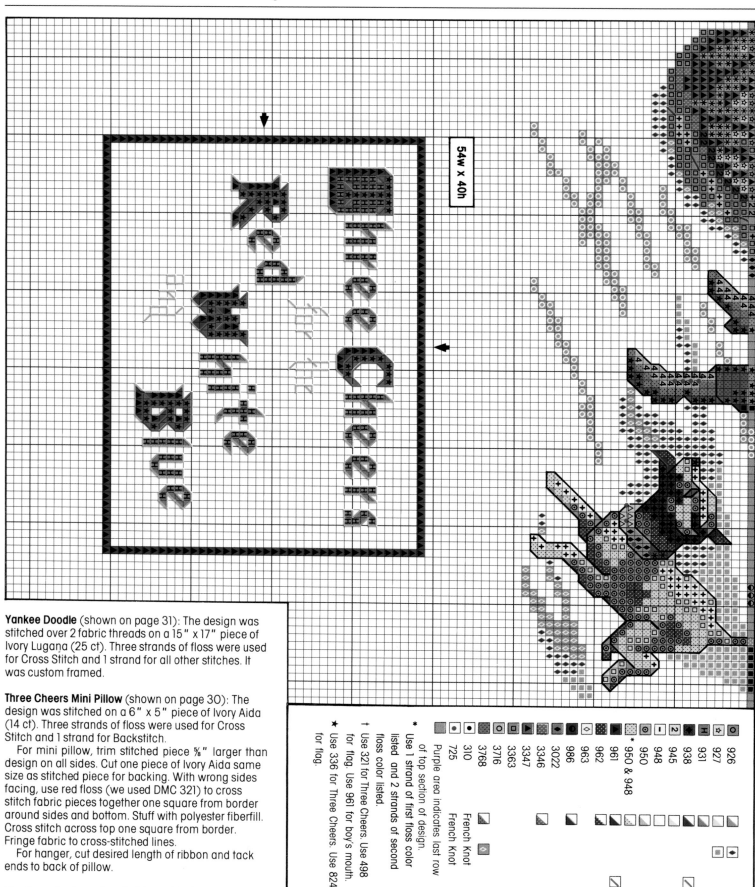

54w x 40h

Yankee Doodle (shown on page 31): The design was stitched over 2 fabric threads on a 15" x 17" piece of Ivory Lugana (25 ct). Three strands of floss were used for Cross Stitch and 1 strand for all other stitches. It was custom framed.

Three Cheers Mini Pillow (shown on page 30): The design was stitched on a 6" x 5" piece of Ivory Aida (14 ct). Three strands of floss were used for Cross Stitch and 1 strand for Backstitch.

For mini pillow, trim stitched piece ⅝" larger than design on all sides. Cut one piece of Ivory Aida same size as stitched piece for backing. With wrong sides facing, use red floss (we used DMC 321) to cross stitch fabric pieces together one square from border around sides and bottom. Stuff with polyester fiberfill. Cross stitch across top one square from border. Fringe fabric to cross-stitched lines.

For hanger, cut desired length of ribbon and tack ends to back of pillow.

Needlework adaptations by Nancy Dockter.

* Purple area indicates last row of top section of design.
* Use 1 strand of first floss color listed and 2 strands of second floss color listed.
† Use 321 for Three Cheers. Use 498 for flag. Use 961 for boy's mouth.
★ Use 336 for Three Cheers. Use 824 for flag.

926
927
931
938
945
948
950
950 & 948
961
962
963
986
3022
3346
3347
3363
3716
3768
310 — French Knot
725 — French Knot

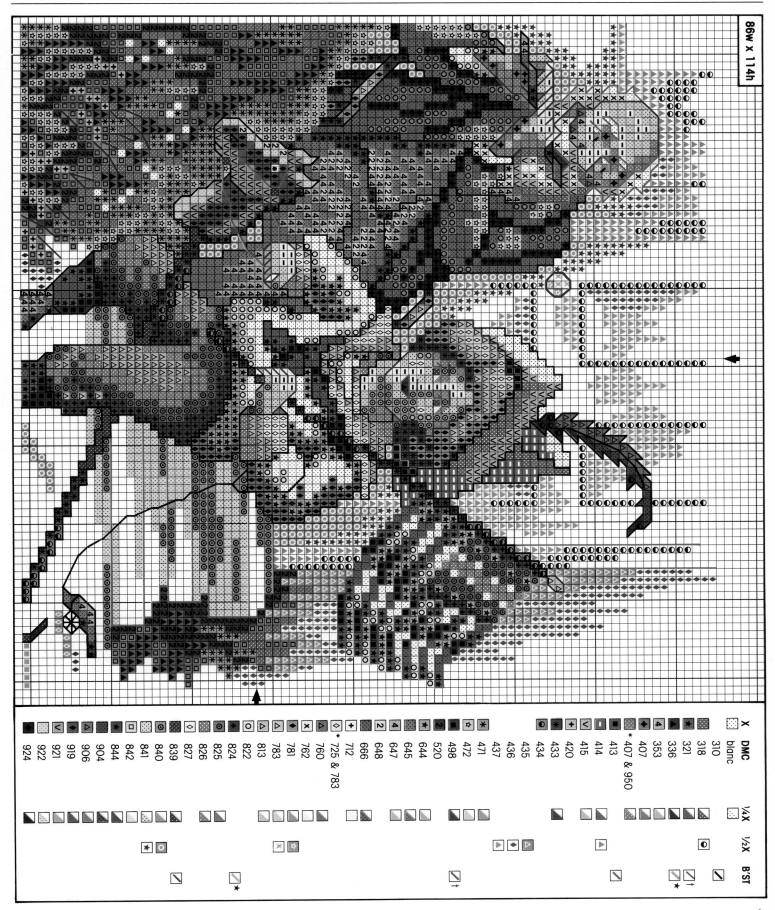

	X DMC		¼X	½X	B'ST
	310				
	318				
	321				
	336				
	353				
	★ 407				
	407 & 950				
	413				
	414				
	415				
	420				
	433				
	434				
	435				
	436				
	437				
	471				
	472				
	498				
	520				
	644				
	645				
	647				
	648				
	666				
	712				
	★ 725 & 783				
	760				
	762				
	781				
	783				
	813				
	822				
	824				
	825				
	826				
	827				
	839				
	840				
	841				
	842				
	844				
	904				
	906				
	919				
	921				
	922				
	924				

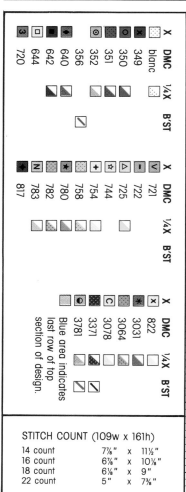

X	DMC	¼X	B'ST
⁘	blanc	✓	
×	349		
O	350	✓	
▒	351	✓	
⊙	352	✓	
	356		✓
◆	640	✓	
■	642	✓	
□	644		
3	720		
V	721		
I	722		
△	725	✓	
☆	744		
+	754	✓	
▒	758	✓	
★	780	✓	
⁘	782	✓	
N	783	✓	
◆	817		
×	822	✓	
✱	3031	✓	
▒	3064	✓	
C	3078	✓	
▓	3371	✓	✓
◐	3781	✓	✓
▒	Blue area indicates last row of top section of design.		

STITCH COUNT (109w x 161h)			
14 count	7⅞"	x	11½"
16 count	6⅞"	x	10⅛"
18 count	6⅛"	x	9"
22 count	5"	x	7⅜"

Witch and Owl Wall Hanging (shown on page 33): The design was stitched over 2 fabric threads on a 23½" x 41½" piece of Floba (14 ct). Six strands of floss were used for Cross Stitch and 2 strands for Backstitch.

For wall hanging, center design horizontally with the bottom of the design 8½" from one short edge of fabric piece. Measure 4½" from bottom edge of fabric and pull out one fabric thread. Fringe up to missing fabric thread. On each side, turn fabric under ½" and press; turn fabric under ½" again and hem. For casing at top edge, turn fabric under 1" and press; turn fabric under 3" and hem.

Needlework adaptation by Carol Emmer.

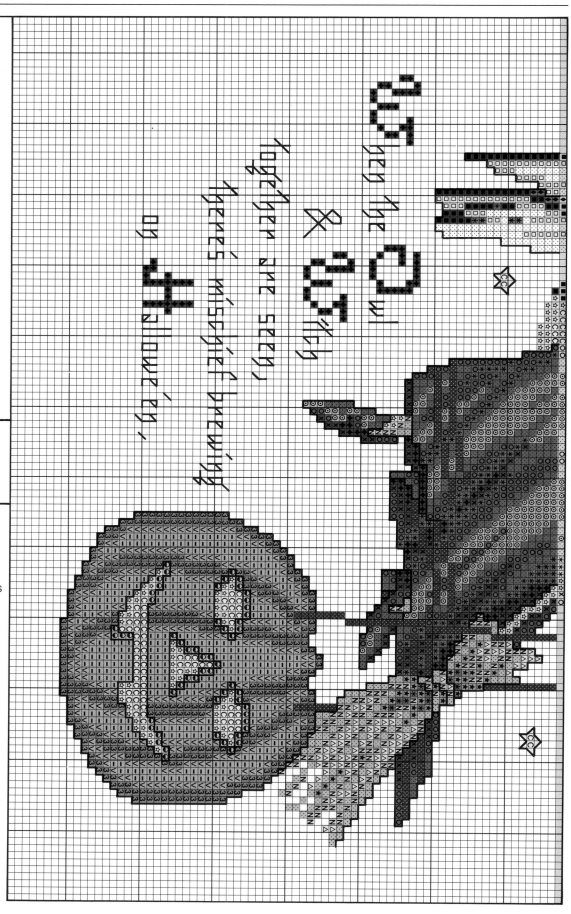

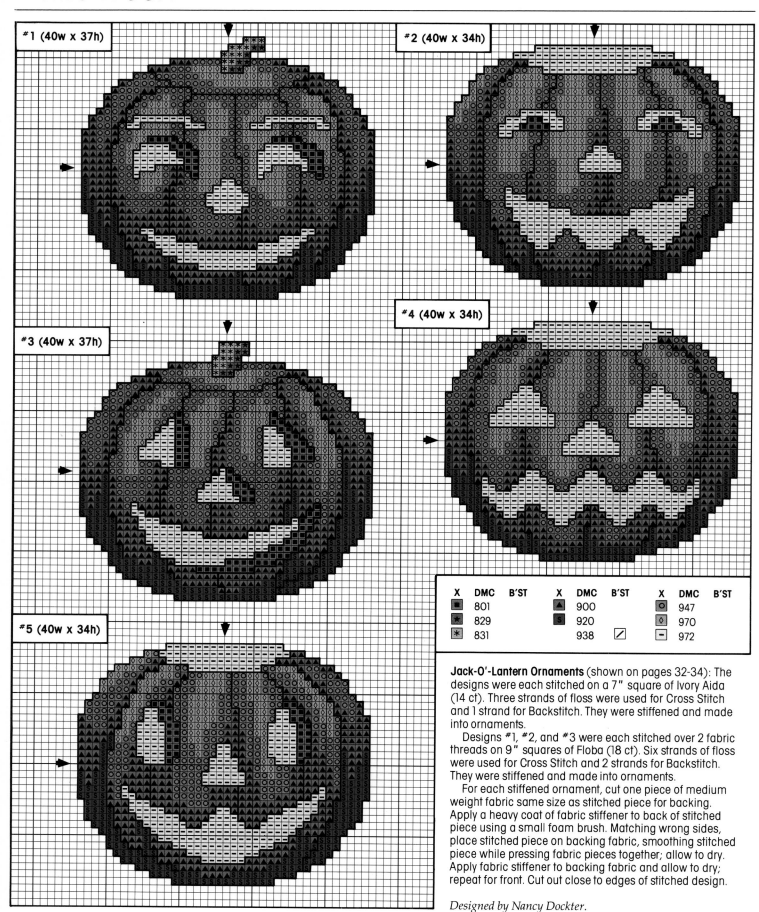

#1 (40w x 37h)

#2 (40w x 34h)

#4 (40w x 34h)

#3 (40w x 37h)

#5 (40w x 34h)

X	DMC	B'ST	X	DMC	B'ST	X	DMC	B'ST
■	801		▲	900		◉	947	
★	829		S	920		◇	970	
✳	831			938	/	−	972	

Jack-O'-Lantern Ornaments (shown on pages 32-34): The designs were each stitched on a 7" square of Ivory Aida (14 ct). Three strands of floss were used for Cross Stitch and 1 strand for Backstitch. They were stiffened and made into ornaments.

Designs #1, #2, and #3 were each stitched over 2 fabric threads on 9" squares of Floba (18 ct). Six strands of floss were used for Cross Stitch and 2 strands for Backstitch. They were stiffened and made into ornaments.

For each stiffened ornament, cut one piece of medium weight fabric same size as stitched piece for backing. Apply a heavy coat of fabric stiffener to back of stitched piece using a small foam brush. Matching wrong sides, place stitched piece on backing fabric, smoothing stitched piece while pressing fabric pieces together; allow to dry. Apply fabric stiffener to backing fabric and allow to dry; repeat for front. Cut out close to edges of stitched design.

Designed by Nancy Dockter.

63w x 43h

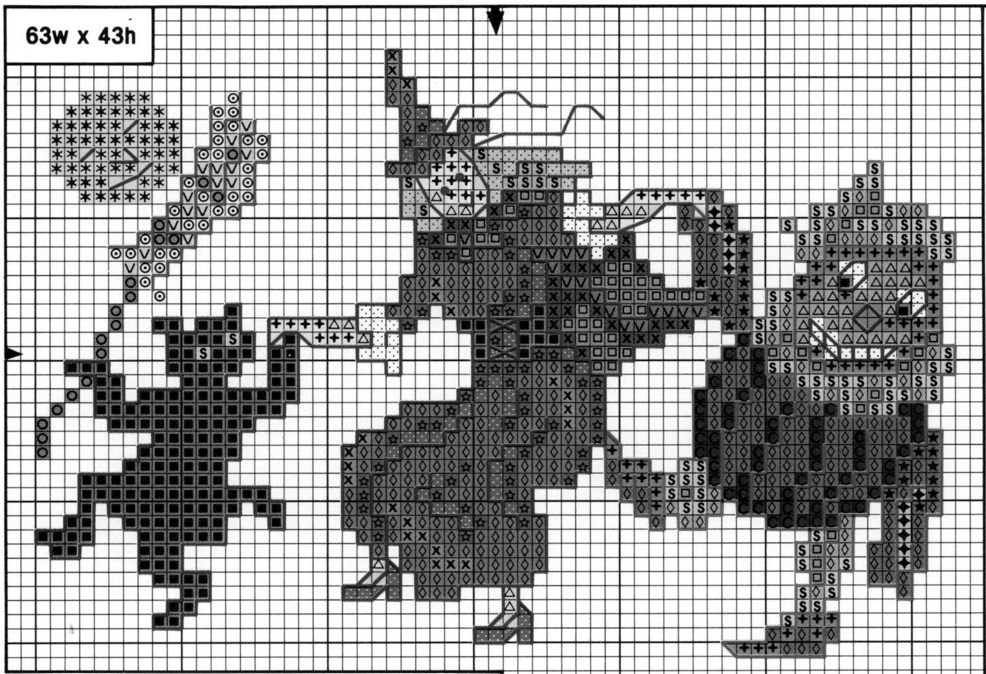

X	DMC	¼X	B'ST	X	DMC	¼X	B'ST
▫	blanc	◩		■	729	◩	
■	304			+	742		
■	310		/	*	743		
■	347	◩		-	746		
◊	349	◩		△	754	◩	
x	350			▫	758	◩	
-	351			O	801		
■	353			☆	817		
■	420			2	822		
◊	422				839		/
V	435			◊	900		
⊙	437			x	904		
■	469	◩		□	905		
*	470			◊	906		
C	471			C	920		
-	472			■	935	◩	
	632	◩	/	▲	936		
■	640			+	947	◩	
☆	642			+	948	◩	
x	644			△	970		
S	645			*	3064	◩	
▫	647			S	3328	◩	
◊	676	◩		V	3345		
O	677				3346		/
x	680				3371		/
S	704			•	310 French Knot		

Halloween Dance Mug (shown on page 35): The design was centered horizontally and stitched (omitting Quarter Stitches) 3 squares from the bottom of a 10¼" x 3½" piece of Vinyl-Weave® (14 ct). It was inserted in a Stitch-A-Mug™. Three strands of floss were used for Cross Stitch and 1 strand for all other stitches.

Halloween Dance Shirt (shown on page 37): The design was stitched over a 10" x 8" piece of 11 mesh waste canvas on a child's sweatshirt. Four strands of floss were used for Cross Stitch and 2 strands for all other stitches. (See Working on Waste Canvas, page 75.)

Needlework adaptation by Linda Culp Calhoun.

96w x 54h

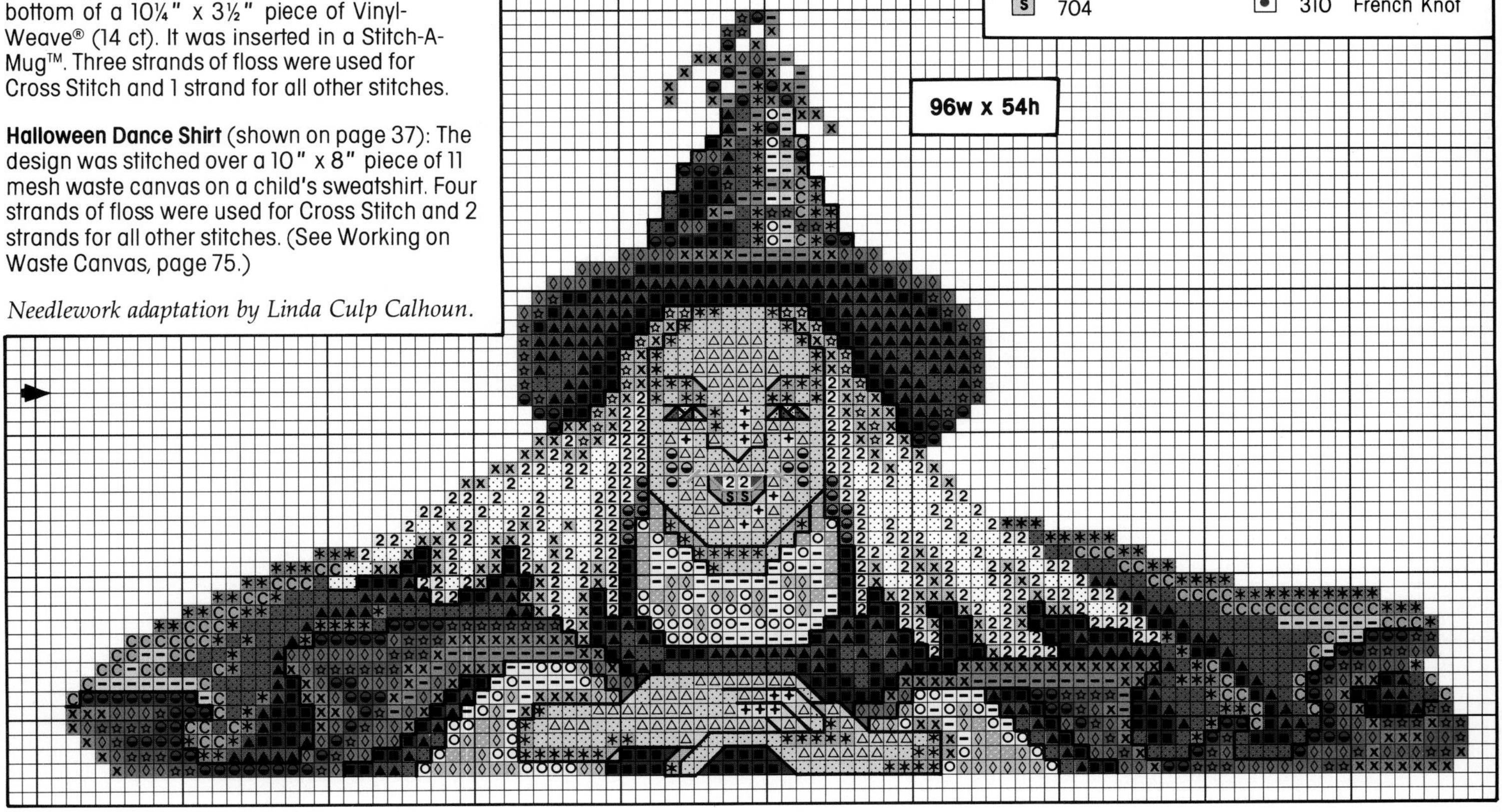

Witch Basket Ornament (shown on page 35): The design was stitched on a 13" x 10" piece of Antique White Aida (14 ct). Three strands of floss were used for Cross Stitch and 1 strand for Backstitch.

For ornament, cut one 13" x 10" piece of Antique White Aida for backing. With right sides facing and leaving an opening at bottom edge for turning and stuffing, sew stitched piece and backing fabric together ¼" from edge of design. Leaving a ¼" seam allowance, cut out ornament; clip curves and turn right side out. Stuff with polyester fiberfill. Sew final closure by hand.

Refer to photo and hot glue ornament to edge of basket.

Needlework adaptation by Carol Emmer.

halloween

Needlework adaptations by Linda Culp Calhoun.

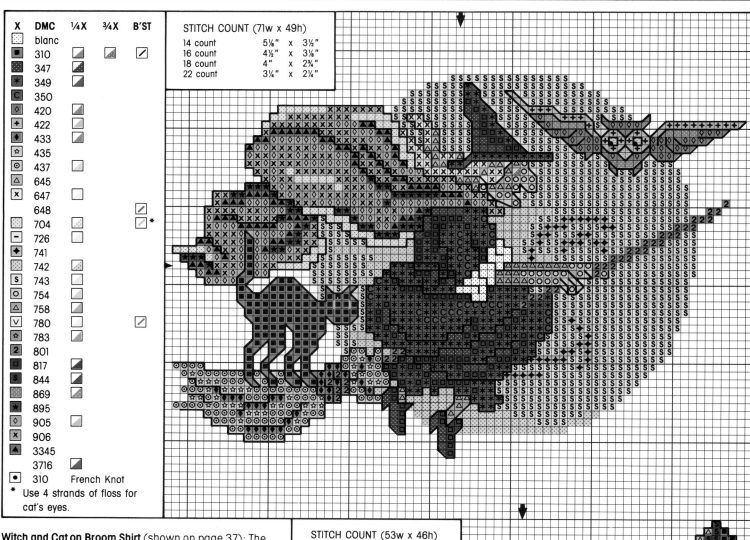

X	DMC	1/4X	3/4X	B'ST
	blanc			
■	310	◢	◿	◿
	347	◢		
*	349	◢		
C	350			
◇	420	◢		
✦	422	◢		
◆	433	◢		
☆	435			
⊙	437	◢		
△	645			
x	647	☐		
	648			◿
	704	◢		◿ *
−	726	☐		
◆	741			
	742	◢		
S	743	☐		
○	754	☐		
△	758	◢		
V	780	☐		◿
☆	783	◢		
2	801			
◘	817	◢		
S	844	◢		
◙	869	◢		
✶	895			
◇	905	◢		
x	906			
▲	3345			
	3716	◢		
●	310	French Knot		

* Use 4 strands of floss for cat's eyes.

STITCH COUNT (71w x 49h)		
14 count	5⅛"	x 3½"
16 count	4½"	x 3⅛"
18 count	4"	x 2¾"
22 count	3¼"	x 2¼"

Witch and Cat on Broom Shirt (shown on page 37): The design was stitched over a 12½" x 9½" piece of 8.5 mesh waste canvas on a purchased sweatshirt. Six strands of floss were used for Cross Stitch, 4 strands for French Knots, and 2 strands for Backstitch. (See Working on Waste Canvas, page 75.)

Cat and Moon Shirt (shown on page 37): The design was stitched over a 10½" x 9" piece of 8.5 mesh waste canvas on a purchased sweatshirt. Six strands of floss were used for Cross Stitch and 2 strands for Backstitch. (See Working on Waste Canvas, page 75.)

For fence, cut one 6" length, one 7" length, and two 13" lengths of ⅞"w grosgrain ribbon. Press short ends of 13" lengths ¼" to wrong side. Press one short end of 6" and 7" lengths ¼" to wrong side. Fold each remaining short end to wrong side to form points; press. For each ribbon, cut a piece of paper-backed fusible web slightly smaller than ribbon; follow manufacturer's instructions to apply fusible web to wrong side of ribbon. Remove paper backing. Referring to photo, place 13" ribbon lengths horizontally on sweatshirt 1½" apart; fuse in place and topstitch close to all edges. Place remaining ribbon lengths vertically on sweatshirt; fuse in place and topstitch close to all edges.

STITCH COUNT (53w x 46h)		
14 count	3⅞"	x 3⅜"
16 count	3⅜"	x 2⅞"
18 count	3"	x 2⅝"
22 count	2½"	x 2⅛"

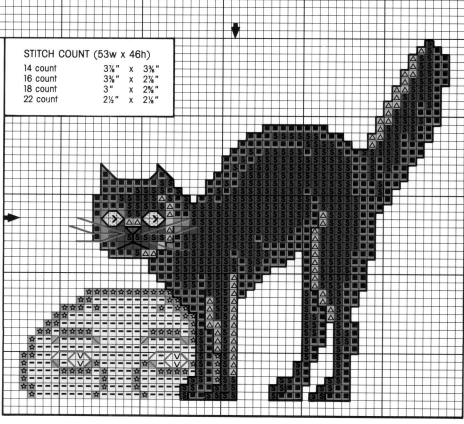

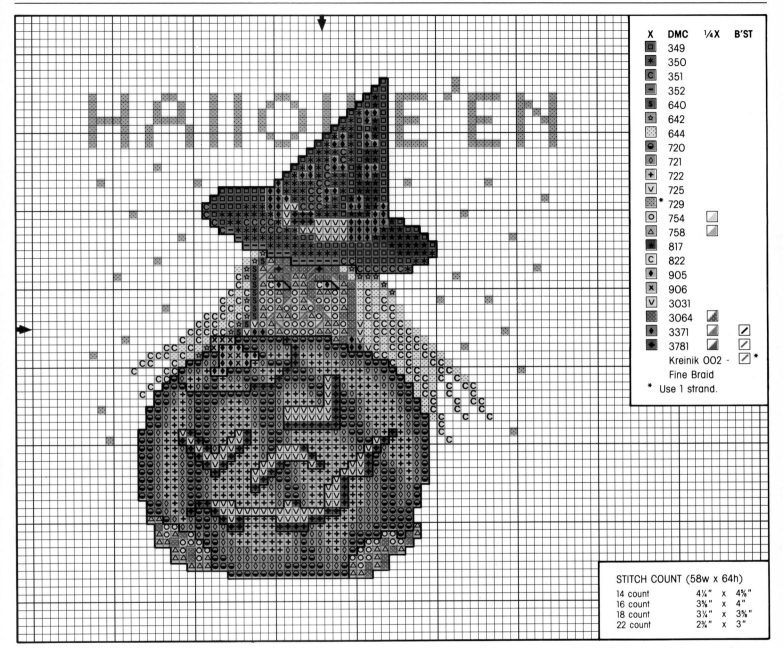

X	DMC	¼X	B'ST
▣	349		
✳	350		
C	351		
▬	352		
S	640		
☆	642		
▒	644		
◉	720		
◈	721		
✦	722		
V	725		
▒ *	729		
⬤	754	◪	
△	758	◪	
◼	817		
C	822		
◆	905		
X	906		
V	3031		
▨	3064	◪	
◆	3371	◪	✎
◈	3781	◪	✎
	Kreinik 002 -		✎ *
	Fine Braid		
	* Use 1 strand.		

STITCH COUNT (58w x 64h)

14 count	4¼"	x 4⅝"
16 count	3⅝"	x 4"
18 count	3¼"	x 3⅝"
22 count	2¾"	x 3"

Witch and Pumpkin Shirt (shown on page 36): The design was stitched over a 12" square of 8.5 mesh waste canvas on a purchased T-shirt. Six strands of floss were used for Cross Stitch (except where indicated on chart) and 2 strands for Backstitch. Gold 5mm star-shaped sequins and gold seed beads were added to shirt.

After waste canvas is removed, run needle threaded with 2 strands of DMC 729 up through center of each DMC 729 cross stitch. Thread sequin, then bead onto needle. Run thread back down through hole of sequin. Move to next cross stitch and continue adding sequins and beads .

Needlework adaptation by Carol Emmer.

WORKING ON WASTE CANVAS

Waste canvas is a special canvas that provides an evenweave grid for placing stitches on fabric. After the design is worked over the canvas, the canvas threads are removed leaving the design on the fabric. The canvas is available in several mesh sizes.

Cover edges of canvas with masking tape. Cut a piece of lightweight, non-fusible interfacing the same size as canvas to provide a firm stitching base.

Find desired stitching area on shirt and mark center of area with a pin. Match center of canvas to pin. Use the blue threads in canvas to place canvas straight on shirt; pin canvas to shirt. Pin interfacing to wrong side of shirt. Baste all three thicknesses together as shown in **Fig. 1**.

Place shirt in a screw type hoop. We recommend a hoop that is large enough to encircle entire design. Using a sharp needle, work design, stitching from large holes to large holes.

Trim canvas to within ¾" of design. Dampen canvas until it becomes limp. Pull out canvas threads one at a time using tweezers (**Fig. 2**). Trim interfacing close to design.

Fig. 1

Fig. 2

75

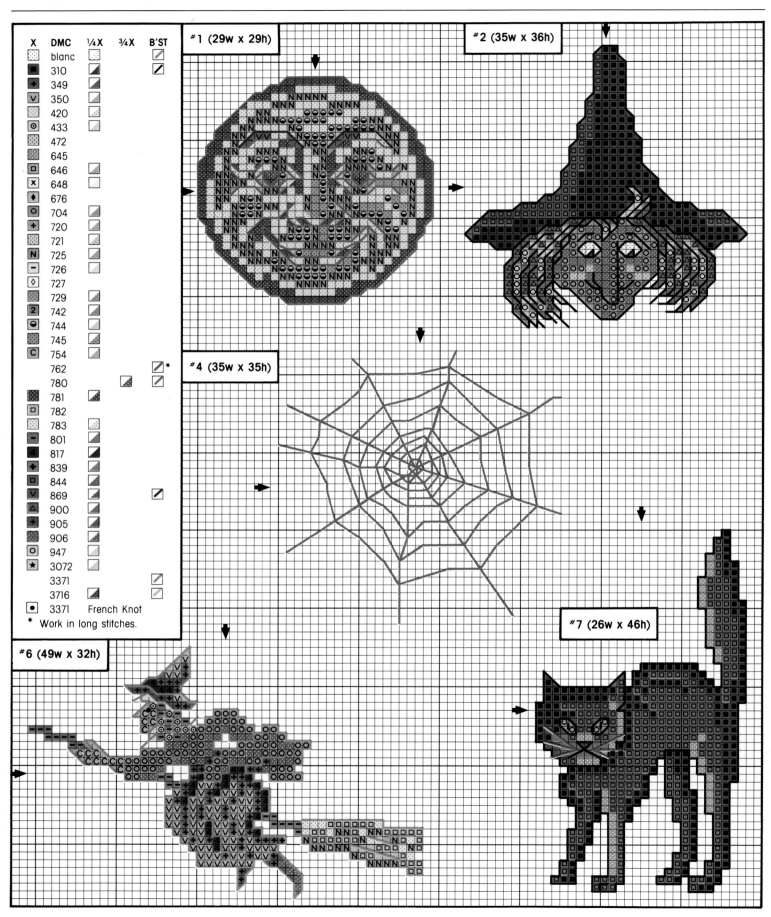

X	DMC	¼X	¾X	B'ST
	blanc			
	310			
	349			
V	350			
	420			
⊙	433			
	472			
	645			
	646			
X	648			
◆	676			
O	704			
	720			
	721			
N	725			
−	726			
◇	727			
	729			
2	742			
	744			
	745			
C	754			
	762			*
	780			
	781			
	782			
	783			
−	801			
	817			
◆	839			
	844			
V	869			
△	900			
	905			
	906			
O	947			
★	3072			
	3371			
	3716			
•	3371	French Knot		

* Work in long stitches.

#1 (29w x 29h)

#2 (35w x 36h)

#4 (35w x 35h)

#7 (26w x 46h)

#6 (49w x 32h)

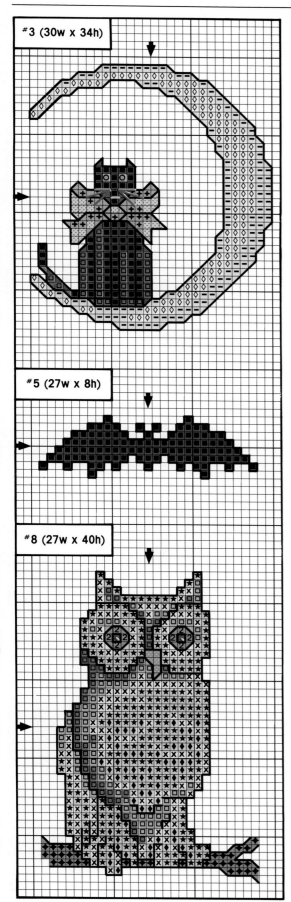

#3 (30w x 34h)

#5 (27w x 8h)

#8 (27w x 40h)

Moon Lapel Pin (shown on page 36): Design #1 was stitched on a 6" square of Ivory Aida (14 ct). Three strands of floss were used for Cross Stitch and 1 strand for Backstitch.

For stiffened lapel pin, cut one piece of cream medium weight fabric same size as stitched piece for backing. Apply a heavy coat of fabric stiffener to back of stitched piece using a small foam brush. Matching wrong sides, place stitched piece on backing fabric, smoothing stitched piece while pressing fabric pieces together; allow to dry. Apply fabric stiffener to backing fabric and allow to dry; repeat for front. Cut out close to edges of stitched design. Glue 1" pin back to back of stiffened piece.

Needlework adaptation by Nancy Dockter.

Witch Candy Bag (shown on page 35): Design #2 was stitched on a 6" square of Ivory Aida (14 ct). Three strands of floss were used for Cross Stitch and 1 strand for Backstitch. The design was stiffened and applied to a candy bag.

For candy bag, you will need fabric stiffener, small foam brush, 6" square of cream medium weight fabric for backing, two 5" x 6½" pieces of desired fabric for bag, one 18" length of ⅛"w ribbon, fabric glue, small safety pin, and liquid fray preventative.

For stiffened design, apply a heavy coat of fabric stiffener to back of stitched piece using foam brush. Matching wrong sides, place stitched piece on backing fabric smoothing stitched piece while pressing fabric pieces together; allow to dry. Apply fabric stiffener to backing fabric and allow to dry; repeat for front. Cut out close to edges of stitched design.

For candy bag, match right sides and raw edges and use a ¼" seam allowance to sew fabric pieces together along three sides, leaving one short side open. Turn raw edge of fabric ¼" to wrong side and press; turn edge ¼" to wrong side again and press. Topstitch close to first fold, making a ¼" casing. Trim seam allowances diagonally at corners and turn candy bag right side out. Cut a small opening in the back center of casing; apply liquid fray preventative to opening and allow to dry. For drawstring, thread ribbon through the center of small safety pin. Insert safety pin into hole in casing; carefully run pin through casing and out same hole. Remove safety pin from ribbon and apply liquid fray preventative to each end of ribbon. Referring to photo for placement, glue stiffened design to candy bag.

Cat on Moon Jar Lid (shown on page 35): Design #3 was stitched on a 6" square of Ivory Aida (14 ct). Three strands of floss were used for Cross Stitch and 1 strand for Backstitch. It was inserted in a large mouth jar lid.

For jar lid, use **outer edge** of jar lid for pattern and draw a circle on adhesive mounting board. Cutting slightly inside drawn line, cut out circle. Using **opening** of jar lid for pattern, cut a circle of batting. Remove paper from adhesive board; center batting on adhesive board and press in place. Center stitched piece on batting and press edges onto adhesive board; trim edges close to board. Glue board inside jar lid.

Spider Web Tie (shown on page 36): Design #4 was stitched over a 5½" square of 12 mesh waste canvas on a purchased tie. One strand of floss was used for design. (See Working on Waste Canvas below.)

Bat Socks (shown on page 36): Design #5 was stitched over a 4" x 3" piece of 14 mesh waste canvas on the cuffs of a pair of purchased socks. Three strands of floss were used for Cross Stitch and 1 strand for Backstitch. (See Working on Waste Canvas below.)

Needlework adaptations by Kathy Bradley.

Mini Pillow Ornaments (shown on page 35): Designs #6, #7, and #8 were each stitched on a 6" square of Ivory Aida (14 ct). Three strands of floss were used for Cross Stitch and 1 strand for Backstitch and French Knot.

For each ornament, cut stitched piece 1¼" larger than design on all sides. Cut one piece of Ivory Aida same size as stitched piece for backing.

With wrong sides facing, use desired floss color to cross stitch fabric pieces together ½" from bottom and side edges. Stuff with polyester fiberfill. Cross stitch across top of mini pillow ½" from edge. Fringe fabric to cross-stitched lines.

Needlework adaptations by Linda Culp Calhoun.

WORKING ON WASTE CANVAS

Cover edges of waste canvas with masking tape. Find desired stitching area and mark center of area with a pin. Match center of canvas to pin. Use the blue threads in canvas to place canvas straight on project; pin canvas to project. Baste canvas to project.

Using a sharp needle, work design, stitching from large holes to large holes. Trim canvas to within ¾" of design. Dampen canvas until it becomes limp. Pull out canvas threads one at a time using tweezers.

thanksgiving

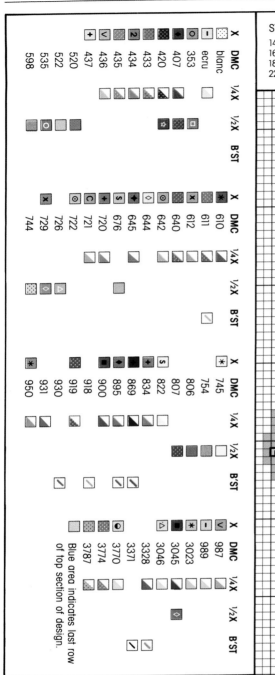

	STITCH COUNT (103w x 148h)	
14 count	7⅜"	x 10⅝"
16 count	6½"	x 9¼"
18 count	5¾"	x 8¼"
22 count	4¾"	x 6¾"

Blue area indicates last row of top section of design.

Pilgrim Woman (shown on page 39) was stitched over 2 fabric threads on a 15" x 18" piece of Cream Belfast Linen (32 ct). Two strands of floss were used for Cross Stitch and 1 strand for all other stitches. It was custom framed.

Needlework adaptation by Nancy Dockter.

X	DMC	¼X	½X	B'ST		X	DMC	¼X	½X	B'ST		X	DMC	¼X	½X	B'ST		X	DMC	¼X	½X	B'ST		X	DMC	¼X	½X	B'ST
	blanc	▨				◎	501	◪				▨	680	◪				▨	900	◪				V	3781	◪		
-	ecru					▢	502	◪				V	720	◪					918			◪★						
	310			◪			517		▨			▢	721	◪	▨			◆	919	◪				* Use 1 strand of each floss				
▲	311	◪	▨	◪			518			◪†		◉	725	◪				▢	930	◪				color.				
▬ *	311 &	◪				◆	610	◪					729	◪				X	931					† Use 518 for eyes. Use 844				
	500					▨	611					◇	739	◪					935			◪		for woman's clothing.				
	318	◪				◉	612	◪				◆	741	◪				▨	937	◪				Use 938 for corn shocks				
	351		◇			☆ *	613 &	◪				*	742	◪				★	938	◪		◪†		and pumpkin stems.				
	352		▨				677					+	746	◪				☆	948	◪				★ Use 632 for faces and				
◕	407	◪					632			◪★		▲	814	◪				▲	950	◪				hands. Use 918 for				
▨ *	407 &	◪				▨	644	◪				▨	815	◪				C	3022	◪		◪		pumpkins. Use 2 strands				
	950					◉	645	◪				◉	816	◪				2	3023	◪				of 3371 for ship masts.				
V	415	◪				+	647	◪				X	839	◪				4	3024	◪								
3	420	◪				C	676	◪				▲	840	◪				▨	3031	◪		◪		**Puritan Relief Ship** (shown on				
*	437	◪				△ *	676 &	◪				▨	844	◪		◪†		▨	3078	▨				page 42): The design was				
C	469	◪					729					★	869	◪		◪		N	3371	◪		◪★		stitched over 2 fabric threads				
N	470	◪				4 *	676 &	◪				+	898	◪					3778	◪				on a 12" x 11" piece of				
	500		◪				744						3779	◪									Cream Belfast Linen (32 ct).					

Two strands of floss were
used for Cross Stitch and 1
strand for all other stitches.
It was custom framed.

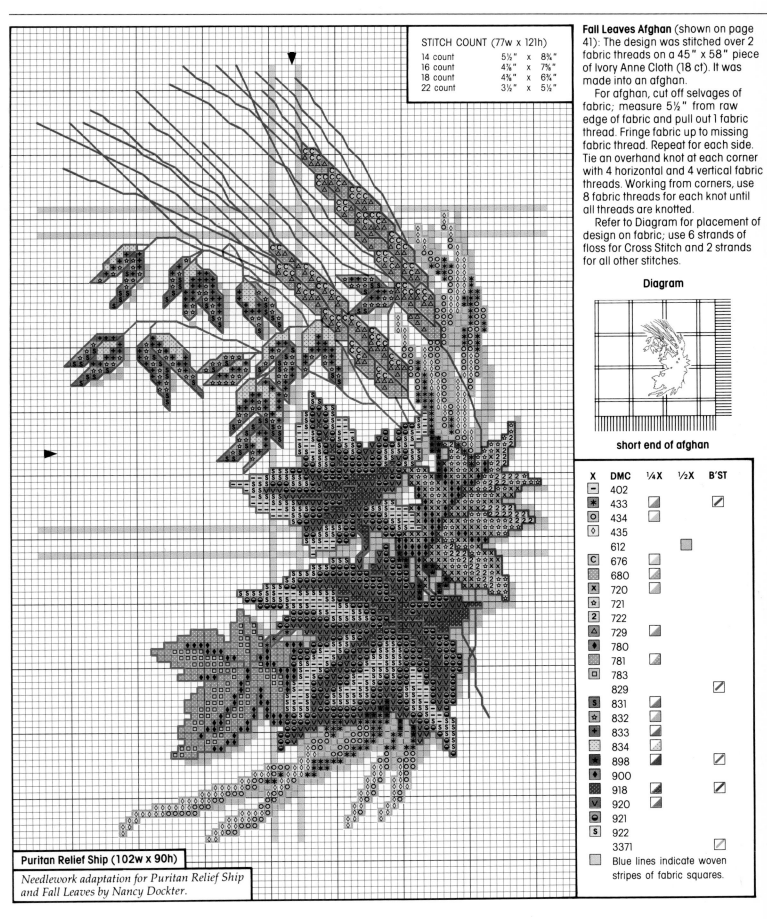

STITCH COUNT (77w x 121h)

14 count	5½"	x 8¾"
16 count	4⅞"	x 7⅝"
18 count	4⅜"	x 6¾"
22 count	3½"	x 5½"

Fall Leaves Afghan (shown on page 41): The design was stitched over 2 fabric threads on a 45" x 58" piece of Ivory Anne Cloth (18 ct). It was made into an afghan.

For afghan, cut off selvages of fabric; measure 5½" from raw edge of fabric and pull out 1 fabric thread. Fringe fabric up to missing fabric thread. Repeat for each side. Tie an overhand knot at each corner with 4 horizontal and 4 vertical fabric threads. Working from corners, use 8 fabric threads for each knot until all threads are knotted.

Refer to Diagram for placement of design on fabric; use 6 strands of floss for Cross Stitch and 2 strands for all other stitches.

Diagram

short end of afghan

X	DMC	¼X	½X	B'ST
−	402			
✳	433	◩		◹
○	434	◩		
◇	435			
	612		▨	
C	676	◩		
▨	680	◩		
X	720	◩		
☆	721			
2	722			
△	729	◩		
◆	780			
▨	781	◩		
□	783			
	829			◹
S	831	◩		
☆	832	◩		
✚	833	◩		
▨	834			
✳	898	◩		◹
◆	900			
▨	918	◩		◹
V	920	◩		
⊙	921			
S	922			
	3371			◹

Blue lines indicate woven stripes of fabric squares.

Puritan Relief Ship (102w x 90h)

Needlework adaptation for Puritan Relief Ship and Fall Leaves by Nancy Dockter.

81

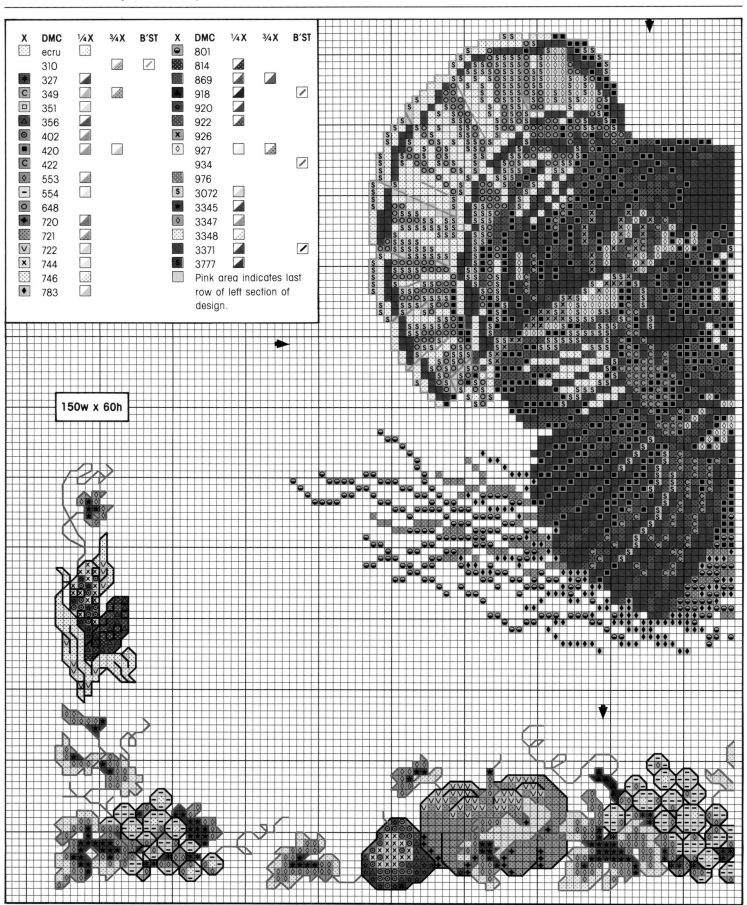

X	DMC	¼X	¾X	B'ST
	ecru			
	310			
	327			
C	349			
	351			
	356			
	402			
	420			
C	422			
	553			
−	554			
	648			
	720			
	721			
V	722			
x	744			
	746			
	783			

X	DMC	¼X	¾X	B'ST
	801			
	814			
	869			
	918			
	920			
	922			
x	926			
	927			
	934			
	976			
S	3072			
	3345			
	3347			
	3348			
	3371			
S	3777			

Pink area indicates last row of left section of design.

150w x 60h

82

STITCH COUNT (99w x 88h)		
14 count	7⅛"	x 6⅜"
16 count	6¼"	x 5½"
18 count	5½"	x 5"
22 count	4½"	x 4"

Thanksgiving Turkey Tray (shown on page 40): The design was stitched over 2 fabric threads on a 12" square of Cream Irish Linen (28 ct). Three strands of floss were used for Cross Stitch and 1 strand for Backstitch. It was inserted in a 12" x 9" purchased tray (10" x 7" oval opening).

Needlework adaptation by Mary Ellen Yanich.

Table Runner (shown on page 43): **Harvest Border** was centered horizontally and stitched across each short end of a piece of Cream Bantry Cloth (28 ct) with bottom of design 2" from raw edge of fabric. (Measure table to determine desired length of fabric.) The design was stitched over 2 fabric threads. Three strands of floss were used for Cross Stitch and 1 strand for Backstitch.

For table runner, machine stitch across each short edge of fabric ½" from raw edges. Fringe to machine-stitched line.

Breadcloth (shown on page 43): The center section of **Harvest Border** design (refer to photo) was stitched over 2 fabric threads on a 13½" x 20" piece of Cream Bantry Cloth (28 ct) with bottom of design 2" from raw edge of fabric. Three strands of floss were used for Cross Stitch and 1 strand for Backstitch.

For breadcloth, machine stitch across each short edge of fabric ½" from raw edges. Fringe to machine-stitched line.

Candle Band (shown on page 43): The grapes and leaves from center of **Harvest Border** design (refer to photo) were centered and stitched over 2 fabric threads on a 12" x 6" piece of Cream Bantry Cloth (28 ct). Three strands of floss were used for Cross Stitch and 1 strand for Backstitch.

(**Note:** We used a candle measuring 2¾" in diameter. If using a different size candle, measurements for candle band will need to be adjusted.)

Matching right sides and long edges fold stitched piece in half. Using a ½" seam allowance, sew long edges together. Turn stitched piece right side out. Press flat with seam centered on back and design centered on front.

For cording, cut two 12" lengths of ⅛" dia. purchased cord and two 12" x 1¼" strips of Bantry Cloth. Center one length of purchased cord on one strip of fabric; matching raw edges, fold strip over cord. Using zipper foot, baste along length of strip close to cord. Repeat for remaining lengths of cord and fabric.

Referring to photo, topstitch one length of cording to each long edge of stitched piece. Turn each short end to back of stitched piece 1"; whipstitch in place. Wrap candle band around candle and whipstitch short ends together.

Napkin (shown on page 43): The grapes and leaves from left corner of **Harvest Border** design (refer to photo) were stitched over 2 fabric threads in corner of a 13½" square of Cream Bantry Cloth (28 ct) 1¾" from raw edges of fabric. Three strands of floss were used for Cross Stitch and 1 strand for Backstitch.

For napkin, trim selvages and machine stitch around fabric ½" from all edges. Fringe to machine-stitched lines.

Harvest Border designed by Jorja Hernandez, Kooler Design Studio.

Christmas

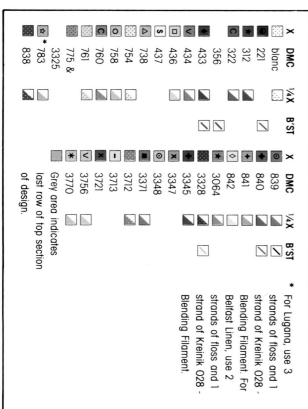

STITCH COUNT (94w x 135h)			
14 count	6¾"	x	9¾"
16 count	5⅞"	x	8½"
18 count	5¼"	x	7½"
22 count	4⅜"	x	6¼"

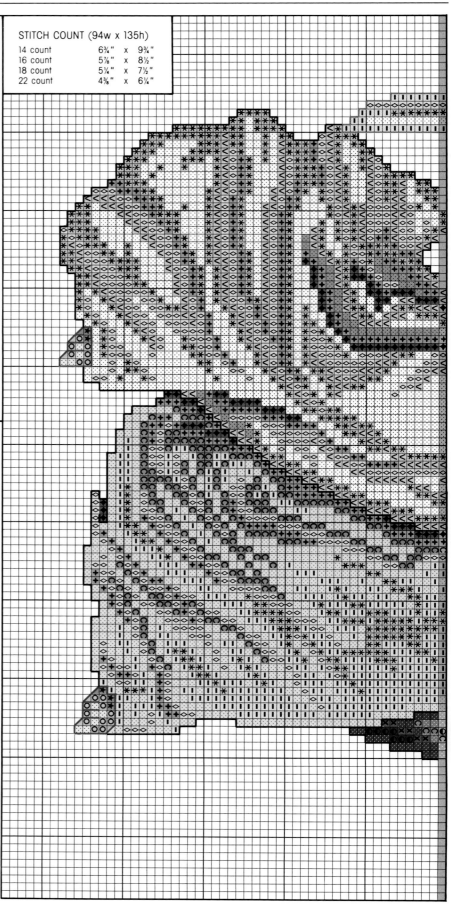

Peace on Earth Angels in Frame (shown on page 46): The design was stitched over 2 fabric threads on a 15" x 18" piece of Cream Lugana (25 ct). Three strands of floss were used for Cross Stitch and 1 strand for Backstitch. It was inserted in an oval purchased frame (11" x 14" opening).

Peace on Earth Angels Pillow (shown on page 49): The design was stitched over 2 fabric threads on a 15" square of Cream Belfast Linen (32 ct). Two strands of floss were used for Cross Stitch and 1 strand for Backstitch.

PILLOW FINISHING
For pillow, you will need a 13" square of ivory fabric for pillow top lining, a 13" square of desired fabric for pillow back, 1½ yds of ⅜" dia. ivory satin cording with attached seam allowance, 1½ yds of ⅛" dia. gold cording, four 3" tassels, and polyester fiberfill.

With design centered, trim stitched piece to measure 13" square. Baste lining fabric to wrong side of stitched piece close to raw edges. If needed, trim seam allowance of ivory cording to ½". Matching raw edges and beginning and ending at bottom center of stitched piece, baste cording to right side of stitched piece.

With right sides facing and leaving an opening at bottom for turning, use a zipper foot and a ½" seam allowance to sew stitched piece and backing fabric together; trim seam allowances diagonally at corners. Turn pillow right side out, carefully pushing corners outward.

Referring to photo for placement and beginning and ending in same place as satin cording, whipstitch gold cording to pillow top. To secure ends of gold cording, remove several stitches and insert ends in opening; hand sew cordings in place. Stuff pillow with polyester fiberfill and sew final closure by hand. Sew tassel to each corner.

Needlework adaptation by Carol Emmer.

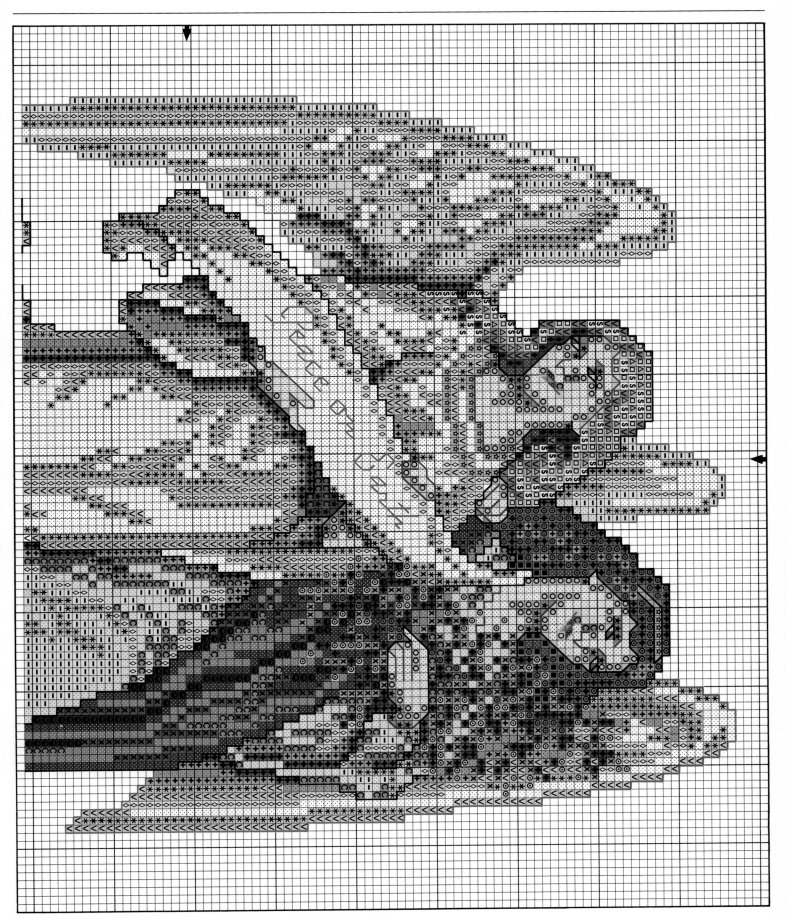

Angel Ornaments (shown on pages 44-45): The designs were each stitched over 2 fabric threads on a 7" x 9" piece of Cream Irish Linen (36 ct). Two strands of floss were used for Cross Stitch and 1 strand for Backstitch. They were made into ornaments.

For each ornament, you will need tracing paper, 7" x 9" piece of Cream Irish Linen for backing fabric, 10" x 7" piece of adhesive board, 10" x 7" piece of batting, 18" length of ¼" dia. ivory satin cording with attached seam allowance, 18" length of ⅜"w gold trim, 3" tassel, 14" length of ½"w gold wire-edged ribbon, and 6½" length of ⅛" dia. gold cording for hanger.

Trace oval pattern (page 92) onto tracing paper; cut out pattern. Draw around pattern twice on adhesive board and twice on batting; cut out. Remove paper from adhesive board and stick one batting piece on each adhesive board piece.

Center oval pattern over stitched piece; pin in place. Cut out stitched piece ½" larger than pattern on all sides; remove pattern. Cut out backing fabric same size as stitched piece. Center stitched piece right side up on top of batting; smoothly fold and glue edges to back of board clipping into edges of fabric as needed. Repeat with backing fabric and remaining adhesive board piece for ornament back.

Glue cording seam allowance to wrong side of ornament front beginning at bottom of oval. Glue ends of cording to wrong side of ornament front and trim ends if needed. Referring to photo for placement, glue ⅜"w trim to back of ornament front beginning at bottom of oval. Overlap ends and trim if needed. Glue tassel to wrong side of ornament front at bottom of oval. For hanger, glue ends of gold cording to wrong side of ornament front at top of oval.

Glue wrong sides of ornament front and back together. Weight with a heavy book until glue is dry. Tie wire-edged ribbon in a bow and glue to bottom of ornament; trim ends as desired.

Needlework adaptation by Carol Emmer.

Angel Porcelain Jar (shown on page 48): The design was stitched over 2 fabric threads on an 8" square of Cream Belfast Linen (32 ct). Two strands of floss were used for Cross Stitch and 1 strand for Backstitch. It was inserted in the lid of a 5" dia. porcelain jar (3½" dia. opening).

Designed by Carol Emmer.

43w x 70h

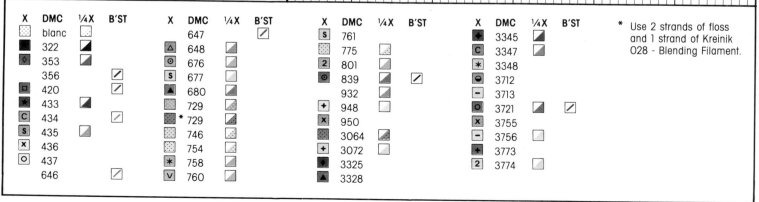

X	DMC	¼X	B'ST		X	DMC	¼X	B'ST		X	DMC	¼X	B'ST		X	DMC	¼X	B'ST		X	DMC	¼X	B'ST
	blanc					647		✓		s	761					3345				*	Use 2 strands of floss
■	322				▲	648					775				C	3347					and 1 strand of Kreinik
◇	353				◉	676				2	801				*	3348					028 - Blending Filament.
	356		✓		s	677				◉	839		✓		⊖	3712					
▫	420		✓		▲	680					932				−	3713					
★	433					729				+	948				◉	3721		✓			
C	434		✓		*	729				x	950				x	3755					
s	435					746					3064				−	3756					
x	436					754				+	3072				+	3773					
◉	437				*	758				◆	3325				2	3774					
	646		✓		V	760				▲	3328										

38w x 71h

43w x 67h

42w x 34h

Christmas

Gloria Angel Stocking (shown on page 47): The design was stitched over 2 fabric threads on a 17" x 21" piece of Cream Lugana (25 ct) with top of design 8" from one short edge of fabric. Three strands of floss were used for Cross Stitch and 1 strand for Backstitch. (See Stocking Finishing, page 90.)

Gloria Angel Pillow (shown on page 49): The design was stitched over 2 fabric threads on a 10" x 14" piece of Cream Irish Linen (36 ct). Two strands of floss were used for Cross Stitch and 1 strand for Backstitch. It was applied to a custom made pillow. (See Pillow Finishing below.)

PILLOW FINISHING

For pillow, you will need, a 7½" x 11½" piece of ivory fabric for lining stitched piece, two 3¼" x 11½" strips of ivory fabric, two 17" x 11½" pieces of fabric for pillow front and back, 1⅔ yds of ½" dia. purchased cord, 2½" x 1⅔ yds bias strip of fabric for cording, polyester fiberfill, and two 11½" lengths of each of the following: ¼" dia. ivory satin cording with attached seam allowance, ⅞"w gold trim, and ⅜"w gold trim.

With design centered, trim stitched piece to measure 7½" x 11½". Baste lining fabric to back of stitched piece close to raw edges. If needed, trim seam allowance of ¼" dia. satin cording to ½". Matching raw edges, baste one length of satin cording to right side of stitched piece along one long edge. Repeat for remaining length of cording and long edge of stitched piece.

Matching wrong sides and long edges fold each 3¼" x 11½" fabric strip in half; press. Matching raw edges, lay one folded fabric strip over cording on top of stitched piece and baste together. Repeat for remaining long edge of stitched piece and fabric strip. Using zipper foot and ½" seam allowance, sew cording and fabric strip to each side of stitched piece. Press seam allowances toward stitched piece. Referring to photo for placement, hand sew ⅜"w trim to folded edge of each fabric strip.

For pillow front, center stitched piece right side up on right side of one 17" x 11½" piece of fabric; pin in place. To attach stitched piece to pillow top, sew along center of each fabric strip through all thicknesses.

For fabric cording, center purchased cord on wrong side of bias fabric strip. Matching long edges, fold strip over cord. Using zipper foot, baste along length of strip close to cord; trim seam allowance to ½".

Matching raw edges and beginning at bottom center, pin cording to right side of pillow front making a ⅜" clip in seam allowance of cording at each corner. Ends of cording should overlap approximately 2"; pin overlapping end out of the way. Starting 2" from beginning end of cording and ending 4" from overlapping end, baste cording to pillow front. On overlapping end of cording, remove 2½" of basting; fold end of fabric back and trim cord so that it meets beginning end of cord. Fold end of fabric under ½"; wrap fabric over beginning end of cording. Finish basting cording to pillow front.

Matching right sides and raw edges, use a ½" seam allowance to sew pillow front and backing fabric together leaving an opening for turning and stuffing. Trim seam allowances diagonally at corners and turn pillow right side out, carefully pushing corners outward. Stuff pillow with polyester fiberfill and whipstitch opening closed.

Referring to photo for placement, hand sew one length of ⅞"w trim to each fabric strip covering stitching line.

Needlework adaptation by Carol Emmer.

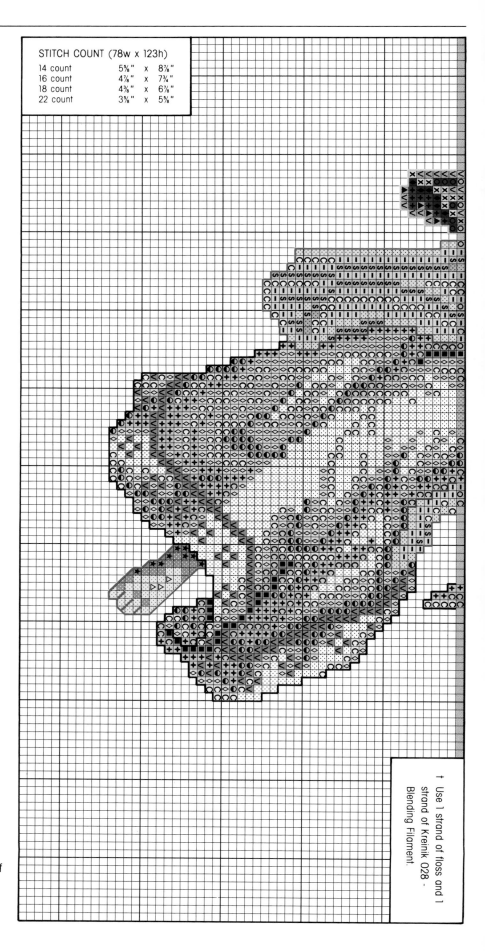

STITCH COUNT (78w x 123h)

14 count	5⅝"	x	8⅞"
16 count	4⅞"	x	7¾"
18 count	4⅜"	x	6⅞"
22 count	3⅝"	x	5⅝"

† Use 1 strand of floss and 1 strand of Kreinik 028 - Blending Filament.

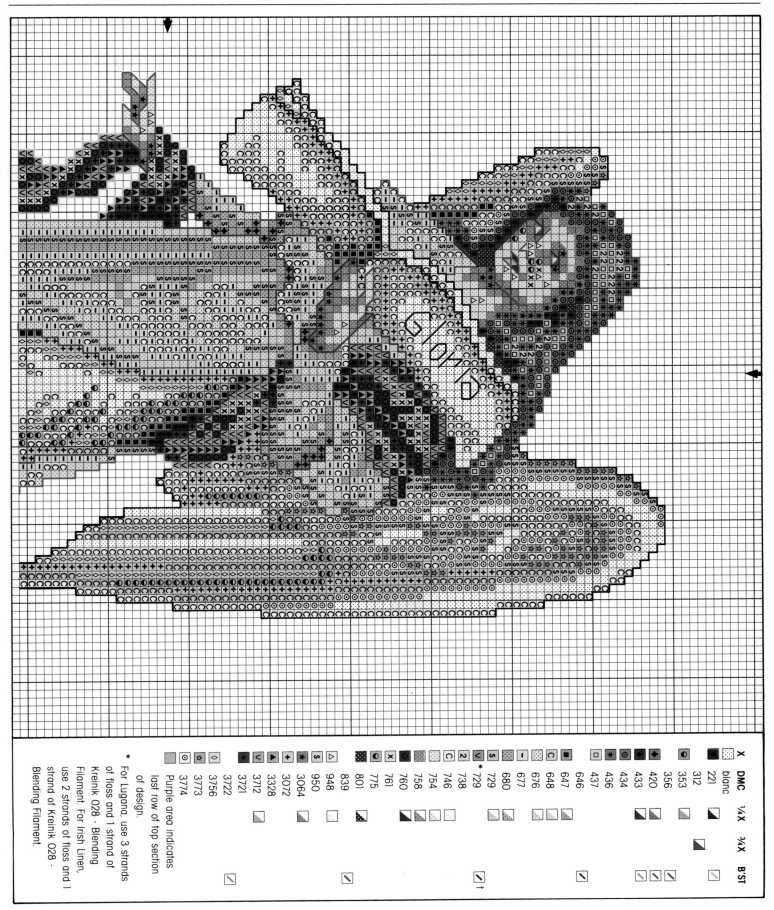

Christmas

Evergreen Angel Stocking (shown on page 47): The design was stitched over 2 fabric threads on a 17" x 21" piece of Cream Lugana (25 ct) with top of design 8" from one short edge of fabric. Three strands of floss were used for Cross Stitch and 1 strand for Backstitch. (See Stocking Finishing below.)

Evergreen Angel Pillow (shown on page 48): The design was stitched over 2 fabric threads on a 10" x 14" piece of Cream Irish Linen (36 ct). Two strands of floss were used for Cross Stitch and 1 strand for Backstitch. It was applied to a custom made pillow. (See Pillow Finishing, page 88.)

STOCKING FINISHING

For stocking , you will need a 17" x 21" piece of Cream Lugana for backing, two 17" x 21" pieces of ivory fabric for lining, a 16" x 10" piece of coordinating fabric for cuff, 36" length of ¼" dia. ivory satin cording with attached seam allowance, 36" length of ⅛" dia. gold cording, 24" length of 1½"w satin ribbon, and 20" length of gold double tasseled cord.

Matching arrows to form one pattern, trace entire stocking pattern (page 92) onto tracing paper; cut out pattern. Matching right sides and raw edges, place stitched piece and backing fabric together. Place pattern on wrong side of stitched piece. Referring to photo for placement, position pattern on design; pin pattern in place. Cut out fabric pieces ½" larger than pattern on all sides. Remove pattern.

Place pieces of lining fabric together. Draw around pattern and sew lining pieces together around sides and bottom just inside drawn line. Trim top edge along drawn line. Trim seam allowance close to stitching. **Do not turn lining right side out.** Press top edge of lining ½" to wrong side.

If needed, trim seam allowance of ivory cording to ½". Matching raw edges and beginning 3" from top of one side of stocking, baste cording to right side of stitched piece, ending 3" from top of other side of stocking. Referring to photo for placement and beginning and ending in same place as satin cording, whipstitch gold cording to stocking front.

With right sides facing and leaving top edge open, use a zipper foot and a ½" seam allowance to sew stocking front and back together; clip seam allowances at curves. Turn stocking right side out.

Matching right sides and short edges of cuff fabric, use a ½" seam allowance to sew short edges together. Matching wrong sides and raw edges, fold cuff in half and press. Matching raw edges, place cuff inside stocking with cuff seam at center back of stocking. Use a ½" seam allowance to sew cuff and stocking together. Fold cuff 4" over stocking and press.

With wrong sides facing, place lining inside stocking; whipstitch lining to stocking.

Tie satin ribbon in a bow; trim ends as desired. Tie tasseled cord in a bow around knot of satin bow. Referring to photo, tack bows to cuff of stocking.

Needlework adaptation by Carol Emmer.

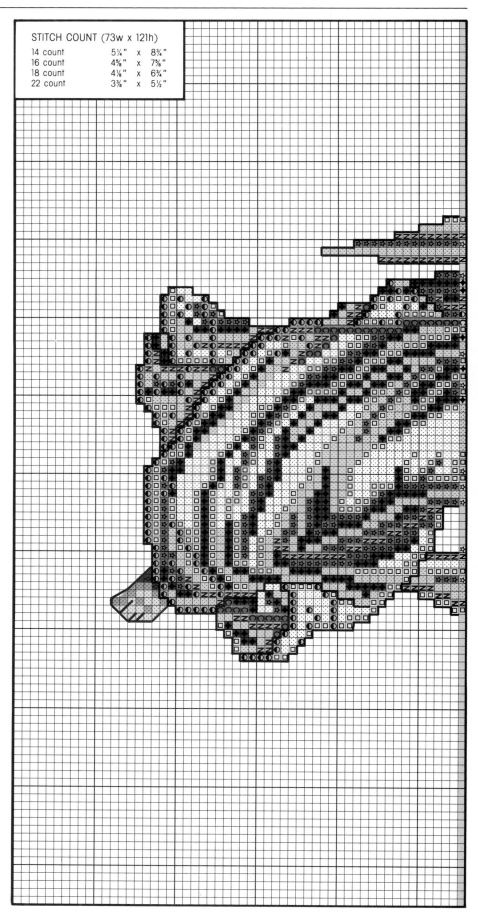

STITCH COUNT (73w x 121h)		
14 count	5¼"	x 8¾"
16 count	4⅝"	x 7⅝"
18 count	4⅛"	x 6¾"
22 count	3⅜"	x 5½"

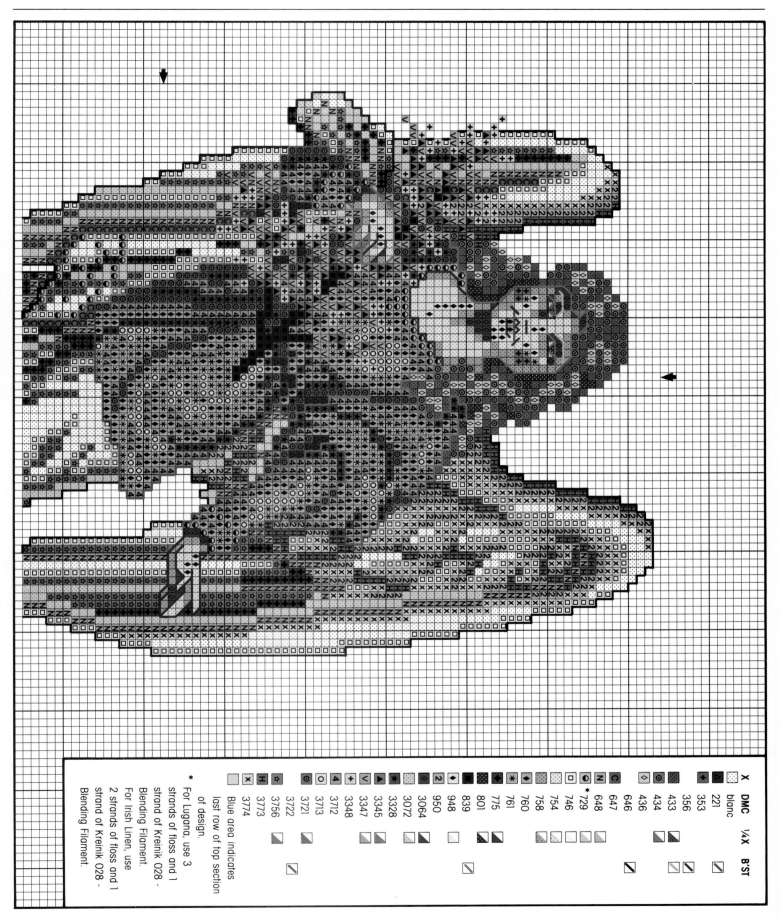

Christmas

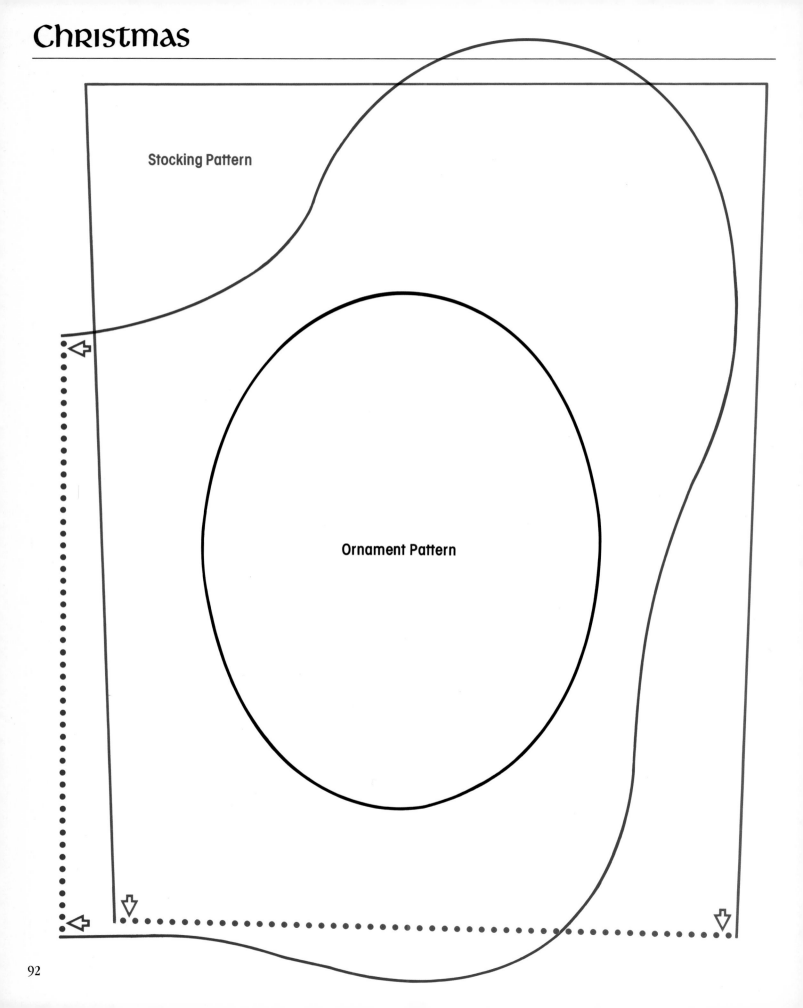

Stocking Pattern

Ornament Pattern

may Day

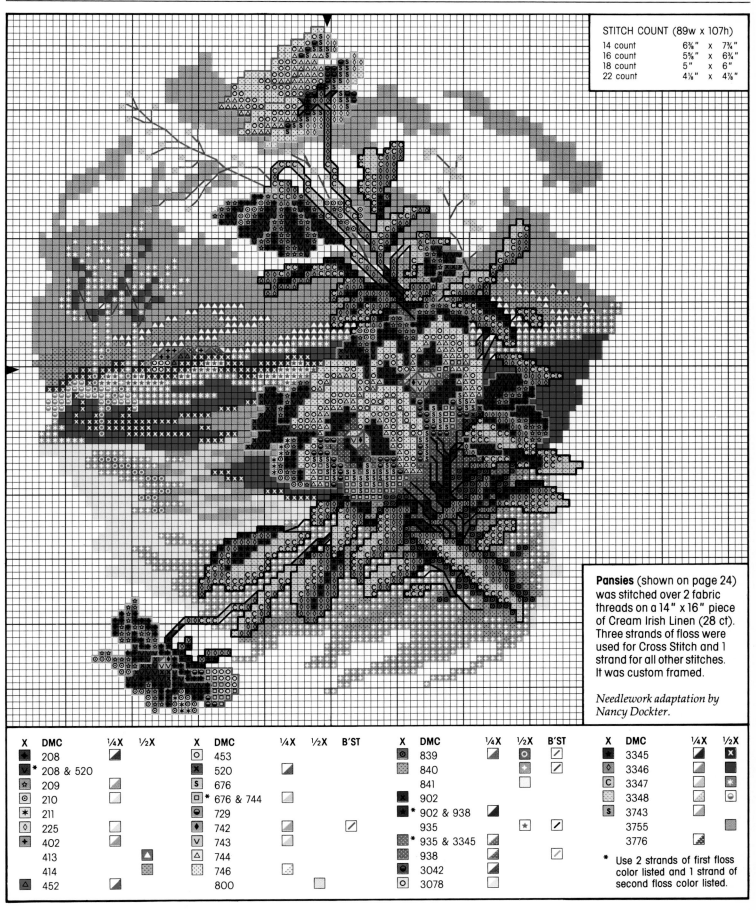

STITCH COUNT (89w x 107h)

14 count	6⅜"	x	7¾"
16 count	5⅝"	x	6¾"
18 count	5"	x	6"
22 count	4⅛"	x	4⅞"

Pansies (shown on page 24) was stitched over 2 fabric threads on a 14" x 16" piece of Cream Irish Linen (28 ct). Three strands of floss were used for Cross Stitch and 1 strand for all other stitches. It was custom framed.

Needlework adaptation by Nancy Dockter.

X	DMC	¼X	½X	X	DMC	¼X	½X	B'ST	X	DMC	¼X	½X	B'ST	X	DMC	¼X	½X
◆	208	◢		○	453				⊙	839	◢	◨	◿	★	3345	◢	⊠
V*	208 & 520			✳	520	◢			░	840		◆	◿	◇	3346	◢	◼
☆	209	◢		S	676					841				C	3347	◢	✳
⊙	210	◻		□*	676 & 744	◢			■	902				░	3348	◢	⊙
✳	211	◻		◓	729				■*	902 & 938	◢			S	3743	◢	
◇	225	◢		◆	742	◢		◿		935		★	◿		3755		░
✚	402	◢		V	743	◢			▨*	935 & 3345	◢				3776	◪	
	413		◬	△	744					938	◢		◿				
	414		░	░	746		◻		◓	3042	◢						
△	452	◢			800		░		⊙	3078	◻						

***** Use 2 strands of first floss color listed and 1 strand of second floss color listed.

93

69w x 107h

X	DMC	¼X	¾X	B'ST
x	209			
C	210			
▣	433		◪	◪
◈	434		◪	
◎	435	◪	◪	
2	436		◪	
–	437		◪	
✦	470	◪	◪	
☆	471		◪	
⊙	472		◪	
★	550		◪	
▲	552		◪	
V	553		◪	
⊟	725			
△	783			◪
	934			◪
★	936	◪	◪	
8	937	◪	◪	
	3371			◪

Grey lines indicate woven stripes of fabric squares.

Violet Afghan (shown on page 26): The design was stitched over 2 fabric threads on a 45" x 58" piece of Ivory Anne Cloth (18 ct). It was made into an afghan.

For afghan, cut off selvages of fabric; measure 5½" from raw edge of fabric and pull out 1 fabric thread. Fringe fabric up to missing fabric thread. Repeat for each side. Tie an overhand knot at each corner with 4 horizontal and 4 vertical fabric threads. Working from corners, use 8 fabric threads for each knot until all threads are knotted.

Refer to Diagram for placement of design on fabric; use 6 strands of floss for Cross Stitch and 2 strands for Backstitch.

Diagram

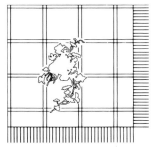

short end of afghan

Needlework adaptation by Nancy Dockter.

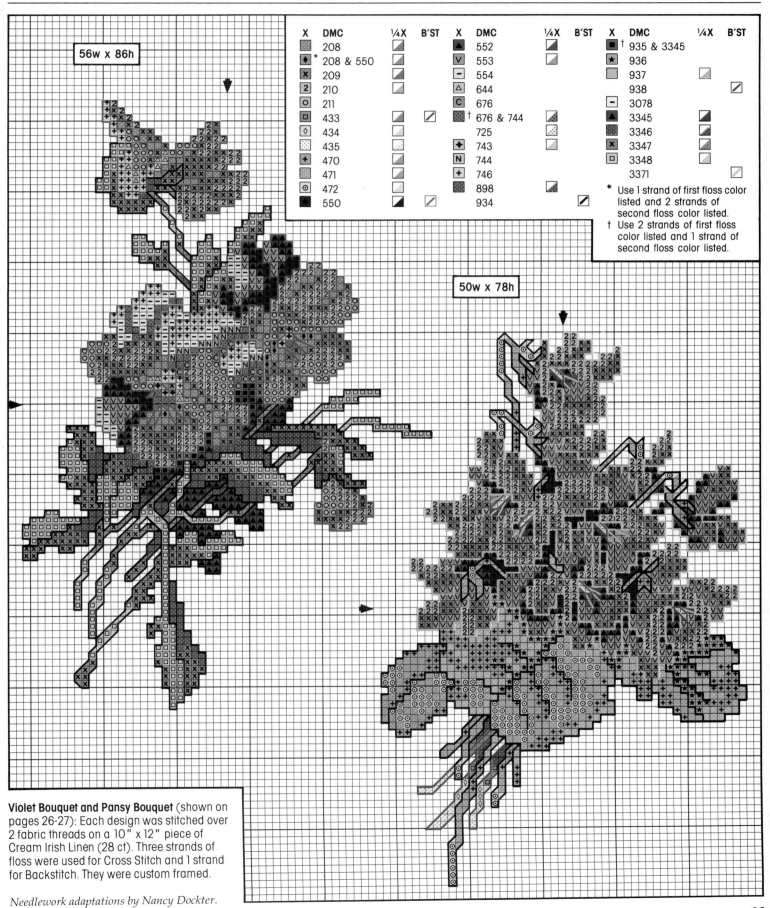

56w x 86h

50w x 78h

X	DMC	¼X	B'ST	X	DMC	¼X	B'ST	X	DMC	¼X	B'ST
	208			▲	552			■ †	935 & 3345		
◆ *	208 & 550			V	553			★	936		
X	209			–	554				937		
2	210			△	644				938		
⊙	211			C	676			–	3078		
▣	433			■ †	676 & 744			▲	3345		
◇	434				725			▣	3346		
░	435			◆	743			X	3347		
+	470			N	744			▢	3348		
+	471			+	746				3371		
⊙	472			▨	898						
✴	550				934						

* Use 1 strand of first floss color listed and 2 strands of second floss color listed.

† Use 2 strands of first floss color listed and 1 strand of second floss color listed.

Violet Bouquet and Pansy Bouquet (shown on pages 26-27): Each design was stitched over 2 fabric threads on a 10" x 12" piece of Cream Irish Linen (28 ct). Three strands of floss were used for Cross Stitch and 1 strand for Backstitch. They were custom framed.

Needlework adaptations by Nancy Dockter.

GENERAL INSTRUCTIONS

WORKING WITH CHARTS

How to Read Charts: Each of the designs is shown in chart form. Each colored square on the chart represents one Cross Stitch or one Half Cross Stitch. Each colored triangle on the chart represents one One-Quarter Stitch or one Three-Quarter Stitch. Black or colored dots represent French Knots. Colored ovals represent Lazy Daisy Stitches. The black or colored straight lines on the chart indicate Backstitch. When a French Knot, Lazy Daisy Stitch, or Backstitch covers a square, the symbol is omitted.

Each chart is accompanied by a color key. This key indicates the color of floss to use for each stitch on the chart. The headings on the color key are for Cross Stitch (**X**), DMC color number (**DMC**), Quarter Stitch (**¼X**), Three-Quarter Stitch (**¾X**), Half Cross Stitch (**½X**), and Backstitch (**B'ST**). Color key columns should be read vertically and horizontally to determine type of stitch and floss color.

Where to Start: The horizontal and vertical centers of each charted design are shown by arrows. You may start at any point on the charted design, but be sure the design will be centered on the fabric. Locate the center of fabric by folding in half, top to bottom and again left to right. On the charted design, count the number of squares (stitches) from the center of the chart to where you wish to start. Then from the fabric's center, find your starting point by counting out the same number of fabric threads (stitches).

STITCH DIAGRAMS

Counted Cross Stitch (X): Work one Cross Stitch to correspond to each colored square on the chart. For horizontal rows, work stitches in two journeys (**Fig. 1**). For vertical rows, complete each stitch as shown (**Fig. 2**). When working over two fabric threads, work Cross Stitch as shown in **Fig. 3**. When the chart shows a Backstitch crossing a colored square (**Fig. 4**), a Cross Stitch should be worked first; then the Backstitch (**Fig. 9 or 10**) should be worked on top of the Cross Stitch.

Fig. 1

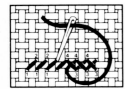

Fig. 2

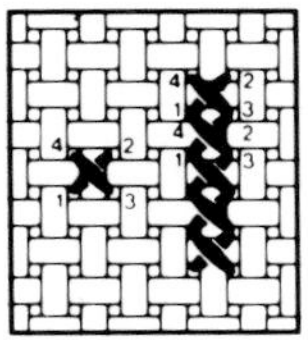

Fig. 3

Fig. 4

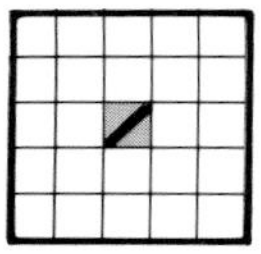

Quarter Stitch (¼X and ¾X): Quarter Stitches are denoted by triangular shapes of color on the chart and on the color key. Come up at 1 (**Fig. 5**); then split fabric thread to go down at 2. When stitches 1-4 are worked in the same color, the resulting stitch is called a Three-Quarter Stitch (¾X). **Fig. 6** shows the technique for Quarter Stitches when working over two fabric threads.

Fig. 5

Fig. 6

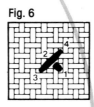

Half Cross Stitch (½X): This stitch is one journey of the Cross Stitch and is worked from lower left to upper right as shown in **Fig. 7**. When working over two fabric threads, work Half Cross Stitch as shown in **Fig. 8**.

Fig. 7

Fig. 8

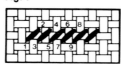

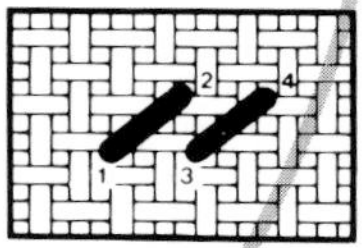

Backstitch (B'ST): For outline detail, Backstitch (shown on chart and on color key by black or colored straight lines) should be worked after the design has been completed (**Fig. 9**). When working over two fabric threads, work Backstitch as shown in **Fig. 10**.

Fig. 9

Fig. 10

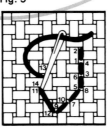
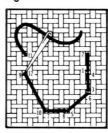

French Knot: Bring needle up at 1. Wrap floss once around needle and insert needle at 2, holding end of floss with non-stitching fingers (**Fig. 11**). Tighten knot; then pull needle through fabric, holding floss until it must be released. For larger knot, use more strands; wrap only once.

Fig. 11

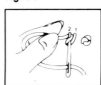

Lazy Daisy Stitch: Bring needle up at 1 and make a loop. Go down at 1 and come up at 2, keeping floss below point of needle (**Fig. 12**). Pull needle through and go down at 2 to anchor loop, completing stitch. (**Note:** To support stitches, it may be helpful to go down in edge of next fabric thread when anchoring loop.)

Fig. 12

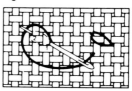

STITCHING TIP

Working Over Two Fabric Threads: Use the sewing method instead of the stab method when working over two fabric threads. To use the sewing method, keep your stitching hand on the right side of the fabric (instead of stabbing the fabric with the needle and taking your stitching hand to the back of the fabric to pick up the needle). With the sewing method, you take the needle down and up with one stroke instead of two. To add support to stitches, it is important that the first Cross Stitch is placed on the fabric with stitch 1-2 beginning and ending where a vertical fabric thread crosses over a horizontal fabric thread (**Fig. 13**). When the first stitch is in the correct position, the entire design will be placed properly, with vertical fabric threads supporting each stitch.

Fig. 13

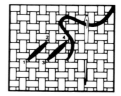

Instructions tested and photo items made by Vicky Bishop, Anne Coppenger, Anita Drennan, Marilyn Fendley, Karen Foster, Joyce Graves, Muriel Hicks, Barbara Hodges, Ginny Hogue, Kathy Kampbell, Susan McDonald, Jill Morgan, Martha Nolan, Wesley Nuckolls, Ray Ellen Odle, Gail O'Nale, Mary Phinney, Susan Sego, Karen Sisco, Debra Smith, Amy Taylor, Michelle Tedder, Karen Tyler, Patricia Vines, Jane Walker, Karey Weeks, Andrea Westbrook, and Marie Williford.